Date Due

NO 8 '61	FEB 25 74	DEC 4 '67	
DEC 11'91	MAR 1 '65		MAR
FEB 2 6	DEC 7		MAR 1 '66
29.9 AG '6 '62	85		FEB 2 7 '67
	MAR 8 1969 69		
JA 2 5 '63			
AR 29 '63	MAR 1 3 '67		
W 8 '63			
SEP 1 6 '63		FEB 1 3 '67	
DEC 1 6			
DEC 1 6 '65		FEB 1 3 '67	
E 1 8 '64			74 NOV 6
MAR 9 '64	MAR 9 '64		
FEB 23 '65	JUN 1 '66		OCT 1 4 1975
JUN 2 4 '66	JAN 26 '66		

Demco 293-5

D1285986

Lincoln and Douglas

The Years of Decision

LINCOLN
AND DOUGLAS
THE YEARS
OF DECISION

———————— ★ ————————

by REGINA Z. KELLY

Illustrated by CLIFFORD GEARY

11347

Landmark
BOOKS

THIS SPECIAL EDITION IS PRINTED AND DISTRIBUTED BY
ARRANGEMENT WITH THE ORIGINATORS AND PUBLISHERS
OF LANDMARK BOOKS *Random House, Inc.* NEW YORK, BY
E. M. HALE AND COMPANY
EAU CLAIRE, WISCONSIN

WITHDRAWN FROM
LIBRARY
FREDERICK R. NOBLE SCHOOL
STATE
WISCONSIN COLLEGE
WILLIMANTIC, CONNECTICUT
EASTERN CONN. STATE UNIVERSITY
WILLIMANTIC, CT 06226

JB
L

6-12-61

Copyright 1954 by REGINA Z. KELLY

*All rights reserved under International and
Pan-American Copyright Conventions*

*Published in New York by Random House, Inc.
and simultaneously in Toronto, Canada, by
Random House of Canada, Ltd.*

*Library of Congress Catalog Card Number: 54-8115
Dewey Decimal Classification: 92*

Manufactured in the U. S. A.

Contents

LIBRARY
FREDERICK R. NOBLE SCHOOL
STATE TEACHERS COLLEGE
WILLIMANTIC, CONNECTICUT

Lincoln and Douglas

The Years of Decision

1. God's Image in Ebony

AN ICY WIND SHRIEKED LIKE A SALEM WITCH hunter along the narrow cobbled streets near Boston's docks and market places. The gas jets flared in the street lamps and almost went out at times. But the sound of the wind was lost in the clop-clop of horses' hoofs, the whir of carriage wheels, the jangling bells of the horsecars, and above all the roar of the people crowding the crooked ways. Angry. Argumentative. Derisive.

New England's silver-tongued orator, Wendell Phillips, was to speak that wild January night of 1854 in Faneuil Hall on the Kansas-Nebraska Bill now being debated in the Senate. Old Peter Faneuil had given Boston a market place near the

3

wharves, and above it a wide hall for a meeting place. Many an impassioned speech had been made from its platform by John Adams and Paul Revere. Now the anti-slavery leaders were taking the stage. For in Boston, people had the will and the courage to fight only if their minds and hearts were won over to a cause.

And what a cause was this Kansas-Nebraska Bill introduced two weeks before by Senator Stephen A. Douglas of Illinois! It provided that two new territories were to be made from the land in the Louisiana Purchase Territory which was north of the parallel thirty-six degrees, thirty minutes. In these two new territories the *people* would have the right to decide whether they wanted their territory to be free or slave.

According to the Missouri Compromise Law which had been passed in 1820, this land was to be "forever free," and so Senator Douglas had also included in his bill a provision for the repeal of the Missouri Compromise. If the Kansas-Nebraska Bill became a law, a new principle

*Those who could not get into the hall huddled
around little fires in the market stalls.*

would be established which would permit slavery to spread into all new territory.

New England was "boiling over." Most of the men and women already overflowing the hall and now jamming the side streets were opposed to slavery. Many were mill hands, clerks, mechanics and small shopkeepers. Some of them had never seen a Negro slave. But the slave was a worker like themselves, except that the fruit of his labor belonged to another man.

Those who were not able to get into the hall huddled, cold but determined, around little fires in the market stalls. They spoke of their work in the mills—the long hours; the poor pay; the dark and filthy rooms in which they worked; the hazards of the machines they used.

"We're not as bad off, though, as the slaves down South," one man protested. "We can quit if we want to. And we can take the money we've saved and buy a farm out West."

"And we've got a chance to rise," said another. "Look at Tom Hooker. He's been made a fore-man. He and his brother are saving to buy a little mill of their own."

But the anti-slavery people were not the only ones attending the meeting. The mill owners, the merchants and the bankers had come from their stately houses on Beacon Hill. They were the ones who bought raw cotton from the planters, who sold them merchandise or loaned them money to finance their crops. They thought that New England and the South were "made for each other." They wanted to preserve slavery because they believed that the labor of free men would increase the price of raw cotton, and, therefore, cut down their profits.

Inside the hall, heads were craned as the people who were to be on the platform now took their seats.

"There's Mrs. Stowe!" came the cry as the author of *Uncle Tom's Cabin* appeared.

There was scarcely anyone in that audience who had not read Mrs. Stowe's book. They had laughed at Topsy's tricks, wept when Simon Legree whipped Uncle Tom, and rushed breathlessly through the pages to see if Eliza would escape the bloodhounds. Nothing that had been written or said had done more than this book to arouse the people against slavery.

7

"And there's Mr. Alcott with his daughter!" cried others as more people came on the platform.

Louisa Alcott stood tall and robust, her dark eyes sparkling with excitement. She was only twenty-one, but her first book of short stories had just been published. There were a hundred more tales that she could tell and play-act in the old house in Concord. But now her tongue and her pen wanted to spill over with burning words against slavery.

A wave of applause greeted John Greenleaf Whittier, for this tall, thin Quaker with blazing eyes and long black hair was the poet of the anti-slavery cause.

Longfellow and Lowell were the next to enter and were applauded generously. The Bostonians knew their writers from Cambridge and Concord. Even the men in the market stalls could discuss the latest literary articles while wrapping a salt fish or a pound of dried beans.

In the beginning it had taken courage for these writers to fight in the vanguard of the anti-

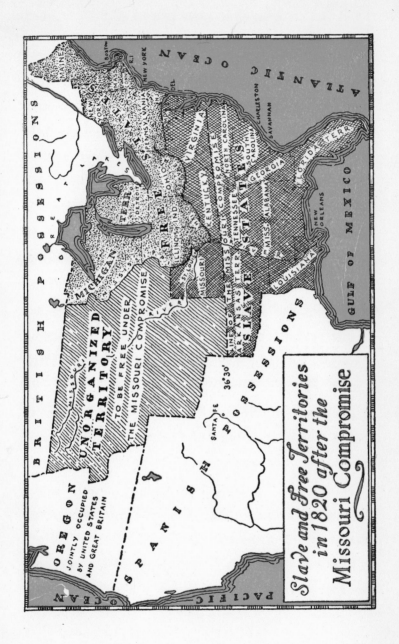

Slave and Free Territories in 1820 after the Missouri Compromise

slavery cause. They were not so well established then. Their books were not bought. Their lectures were unattended. They were denied admission to the Athanaeum, the beloved private library to which all of Boston's literary people subscribed. They were not invited to the social gatherings in the stately houses around aristocratic Louisberg Square. But the writers knew how to suffer for a cause. Most of them were descended from Puritans who had risked sitting in the stocks or having their ears cut off for their religious views.

Finally, all of those on the stage were in their places. The meeting began with a prayer. Then Ralph Waldo Emerson who was to act as chairman introduced Wendell Phillips. Those in the rear of the hall settled back to enjoy a fine two-hour talk.

In the front seats were the people from Beacon Street. They controlled the city government as well as the industries of Boston so they had taken the places near the platform as if by right. Grim and straight, they waited for the speaker to finish;

for later, as in all New England meetings, there would be open debate from the floor. With cold eyes, they regarded Wendell Phillips; for he should have been one of their own since he lived in a fine mansion on Beacon Street. Instead he was the leader in Boston of the Abolitionists, that despised group who wanted to abolish slavery.

The speaker announced briefly that he would give little time to the discussion of the Kansas-Nebraska Bill. He would speak instead on the arguments against slavery. His hearers could follow the debates on the bill in their newspapers. New England lawmakers would vote against the bill, if they knew the voters were opposed to slavery, he said. It was his purpose now to tell them why they should be so opposed.

Mr. Phillips began with a story of a slave auction in Kentucky, a border state where more slaves were raised than needed, and so were often exported. With the splendid diction and dramatic words and gestures for which he was noted, Phillips gave his account.

The owner of a large plantation had died. His

five hundred slaves were to be sold. A rough, burly auctioneer paraded the Negroes on the auction block. He prodded their muscles, opened their mouths to show their teeth, and told of their age, weight, and strength as if they were animals.

One after another, the Negroes were sold to the highest bidder. Families were broken up in spite of weeping protests. The slaves were shackled and herded toward the boats which would take them down the river to the big plantations farther south. Whenever there was a cry or motion of protest, the auctioneer whirled his long black snake whip.

Some who heard Wendell Phillips sobbed openly, but the Beacon Street people snorted indignantly.

Then the speaker raised his hand. This was not the only evil of slavery, he continued. He described the miserable hovels in which the slaves lived, their meager diet of bacon and corn pone, the cruel use of the whip for the slightest offense, the long hours of toil, the laws against teaching a Negro to read.

Scarcely had Phillips stopped, smiling and bowing to the tumultuous applause, when a mill owner from the town of Lowell was on his feet and was recognized by Chairman Emerson.

"Mr. Phillips has grossly exaggerated the evils of slavery in the South," cried the mill owner. "I have visited many plantations. Most of the owners are kind. Their Negroes are docile and affectionate. They live in clean whitewashed cabins. They have plenty of food and can raise vegetables in their own garden patches. The old people and infirm are cared for by the owners. Every self-respecting man in the South would scorn an owner who did not provide for his people."

He paused for breath, but the banker next to him was swift to rise before any of the anti-slavery men on the platform could answer the statements.

"Mr. Phillips talked as if the Southerners were not good businessmen," he cried. "Common sense makes an owner treat his slaves well. They are valuable property. That alone would be his reason for feeding, clothing and housing them well and giving them medical care, even if he had no humanity. If slaves are whipped, it is because that is the only means of punishing a crime. Would you have the owner send a slave to jail and lose the product of his labor? There are laws in the South against maiming and branding slaves, and you can depend upon it, no sensible plantation owner has his slaves whipped to the extent that they are injured. They have to be whipped. They are lazy and impudent and careless."

There were hoots and hisses from the crowd.

But the speaker was quick to reply. "Haven't you ever been whipped as a boy? These Negroes are like small children. They need constant discipline."

The banker's wife rose as her husband was finishing. The men on the platform who had jumped to their feet, reluctantly but politely sat down.

"I have also visited these plantations with my husband," she said, beaming. "Never have I seen a pleasanter relationship between master and servant. The Negro children are the pets of the adults and the playmates of the white children. No one is more adored in a household than a Negro mammy. No servant has more control or importance than a Negro butler. All the Negroes are well-fed and happy. I am sure they would never wish to lead a different life."

Those around her nodded and smiled. But some among the audience in the rear looked either puzzled or unconvinced, for both points of view were right, though so widely different.

Whether the Negro received the treatment as described by Phillips, or enjoyed the comforts which the people from Beacon Street had seen, depended largely on the character of the plantation owner. Fortunately for the slaves, they were well treated in most cases. This was because it was practical if for no other reason. Some plantation owners even hired Irish immigrants to do the work they thought too laborious for their slaves.

However, if an owner was harsh or left his affairs too much in the control of a cruel overseer, the Negro suffered hardships. Although the auction block brought suffering and disgrace, there were just as many instances of masters who in their wills freed their slaves or made provision for their care. There were 260,000 free Negroes in the South. Many had been given their freedom. Others had been permitted to earn it. A large number owned property. Often they were able to purchase the freedom of their wives and children. And so there was some truth in all the statements that had been made.

But as the banker's wife sat down, Wendell Phillips rushed resolutely to the front of the platform. "The plantation owners are kind to their mules and their horses for the same reason they are kind to their slaves," he cried. "They are all beasts of burden. You forget and they forget that the Negro is a human being. He is God's image in ebony! No man has the right to his life and his soul."

Phillips rushed to the front of the platform.

He had made the point that was the basic one in the whole argument—not economics, not humanity, but the right of human freedom in a country whose Declaration of Independence said, "All men are created equal."

By this time, another speaker had joined Phillips on the platform. "You tell us of the good side of slavery," he said to those in front, "because that is all you wanted to see on your visits. You see good in slavery because you are the owners of cotton mills and are the bankers for the South."

"The trade in cotton between New England and the South is our most important industry," answered the Lowell mill owner. "Cotton thread is holding this Union together."

"Then the ties that bind us are no stronger than those threads," came the answer from the stage.

"For shame!" cried another man in the front row. "What would Daniel Webster have said to that? He put the Union first of all."

Daniel Webster! Every New England schoolboy knew Webster's famous orations by heart. "Liberty and Union! Now and forever! One and inseparable!" That's what Daniel Webster had said.

"Daniel Webster is dead," sullenly replied the speaker.

But the audience only faintly applauded his answer. To most of them, Daniel Webster was still a great leader.

"Why can't you forget about slavery?" cried the Lowell man, pressing his advantage. "It will never spread to the North. It's too cold up here to raise cotton, and most of the Negroes aren't skillful enough to work in our mills. Slavery will die out in time, even in the South, because it's not profitable."

"Again, you're forgetting the moral side of the question, sir," answered Phillips from the stage. "Unless we take a stand and say slavery is morally wrong, we're admitting it not only has the right to exist but to spread. Members of the Whig party, like yourself, are for New England's cotton, but we think New England's conscience should be represented as well."

"It's time we have 'conscience' Whigs, as well as 'cotton' Whigs," cried another, stressing the point.

But someone else was bolder. "Neither the Whigs nor the Democrats have the courage to face the issue. They're afraid of losing votes either in the North or the South. What we need is a new party."

"Then join the Abolitionists," urged Wendell Phillips. But there was little response to his plea.

The Abolitionists preached that slavery should be ended immediately with no payment to the slaveholder since he was a criminal for owning slaves. But this was too radical even for the New Englanders. The control of the wealthy industrial leaders was as yet too strong for the majority of people to wish to end slavery on Abolitionist terms. Their only concern now was to keep it confined to the South.

At this time, the two major parties in the country were the Democrats and the Whigs. The Democratic party had been started in 1828 with the election of Andrew Jackson. The Whig party had developed during his administration. Its members were the ones who were opposed to the tyranny of "King Andrew." They took their name from the political party in England at the time of the American Revolution which had been opposed to the tyranny of George III. Most New Englanders were Whigs, for this party most closely resembled the old Federalist party to which they had belonged.

However, both Whigs and Democrats were to be found in every state. Therefore, the leaders thought that it would not be possible to elect a President or stand for an issue which did not appeal to all sections of the country. Even though the North had a larger population and might have won an election, men like Clay and Webster had worked for national rather than sectional interests. They believed that the South would secede if the interests of the North dominated the nation. Above all, they wanted to preserve the Union.

At first the Whigs were a mixture of men of various political beliefs united only in their hatred of Andrew Jackson. However, under the leadership of Henry Clay, they gradually developed certain principles for which the party stood. The Whigs favored a high protective tariff, the re-

LIBRARY
FREDERICK R. NOBLE SCHOOL
STATE TEACHERS COLLEGE
WILLIMANTIC, CONNECTICUT

charter of the United States Bank which was largely controlled by the national government, a system of roads to be built by the national government, and a strong central government.

The Democrats were opposed to the United States Bank and favored a strong state government. But, especially under the leadership of Jackson, the Democrats did not always oppose a high protective tariff or a road-building program at national expense.

The Beacon Street people had been quick to notice the reluctance of the crowd when Phillips had urged them to become Abolitionists. "Stop criticizing the South," cried one man, "or its states will withdraw from the Union."

"Why should we be afraid of what the South will do?" asked a speaker from the platform. "The North has more states—more money— more people—more industries. We don't need the South."

"Oh, yes we do," cried a merchant. "Who will buy our farm products and cotton goods?" He turned to the people behind him. "If we close our cotton mills, some of you will be out of work."

The mill hands in the audience looked at each other in fright. The threat of closing the mills was like a cold grip on their hearts.

Again both sides were right. At that time there were eighteen states in the North with a population of 19,000,000 against fifteen in the South with a population of 12,000,000, one third of whom were slaves. Land was worth five times as much in the North as in the South, and there was not even enough food raised in the South to feed its people and its livestock.

Statistics show that in 1860, the combined rice, cotton, tobacco and sugar crops in the South did not equal in value the hay crop alone in the North. Each year the wealth of the South grew less because the value of its land declined. Because of slave labor, cotton was the best crop to raise in the South. It demanded only unskilled labor. It could utilize the labor of the women and children as well as the men. It kept them occupied, and thereby earning their keep, for nine months of the year.

But cotton wore out the soil, and because the plantation owner depended on slave labor, he could not diversify his crops. Nor did he believe he could use the unskilled Negro in other industries. The South was rich in mineral wealth and other resources, but these were largely undeveloped. Intelligent men in the South were aware of this, but since 1850 they had closed their minds to all arguments against slavery.

They refused to listen because the Abolitionists were constantly referring to the Southerners as criminals and wasters. In defense, therefore, the Southerners tried to prove that slavery was morally good. Their clergymen quoted from the Old Testament to show that God had sanctioned slavery. Their professors lectured on how the Negro had been brought from the wilds of Africa and had been civilized by the white man, or the professors went back into Roman history and insisted that the Negro had been destined from all time to be an "inferior race." Newspapers and books written against slavery were banned. After 1850, few young men of the South attended Northern colleges. With each new attack of the Abolitionists, the spirit of hostility grew.

But Wendell Phillips had one point which would mean as much to the mill hands in the audience as the threat of unemployment. "The Southerners state that the Negro is inferior because he is black and uneducated," said he. "Do you people agree that because a white man has a fairer color and a higher intellect he has the right to enslave the Negro? If that is so, then any of you mill hands before me who hasn't had the chance to be educated should be enslaved for the same reason."

"You're right! You're right!" came the cry from the rear. The laborers who were present might not be able to understand the economics of slavery, but they could appreciate this reason for being opposed to it.

Those on the platform were quick to see that this was a good time to close the meeting. With no attention to the people in front who were shouting to be heard, Mr. Emerson gave the signal for dismissal.

"Write to your Congressmen!" Phillips called to the audience. "Tell them to vote against the Kansas-Nebraska Bill. Write to Steve Douglas. He is one of our own. Ask him why he proposed the bill."

"Because he's like Daniel Webster. He wants to save the Union," shrieked the banker to the crowd now leaving the hall. "If you listen to these wild-eyed Abolitionists, the South will secede and we'll all be destroyed."

"Steve Douglas wants to be President, and he's trying to win the votes of the South. That's why he proposed the bill," cried Wendell Phillips in conclusion.

Then he joined in singing the latest Abolitionist song that was now being chanted all over the hall to the tune of "Oh! Susannah!"

26

Oh, Star of Freedom,
'Tis the star for me.
'Twill lead me off to Canada,
There I will be free.

2. The Little Giant

WHY DID STEPHEN ARNOLD DOUGLAS PROPOSE the Kansas-Nebraska Bill—a bill which would allow slavery to spread into every new state in the Union? As the New Englanders said, he was one of their own. Then why did he favor the extension of slavery?

Stephen was born in Brandon, Vermont, on April 23, 1813. His family had lived in New England since 1645, and his grandfather had fought with Washington at Valley Forge. Stephen's father, who was a doctor, died of a heart attack when his son was a few weeks old. Stephen almost died at the same time, for when Dr. Douglas collapsed, he was holding his infant son on his lap. If a neighbor had not rescued Stephen, he might have rolled into the fire.

After the death of Dr. Douglas, Stephen, his sister Sarah, and his mother lived on the farm which Mrs. Douglas had inherited jointly with her brother Edward who was a bachelor. The uncle had promised that Stephen would be educated to be a doctor. But when Edward married and had his first child, he insisted that his nephew should go to work.

Stephen, who loved carpentry, was an apprentice to a cabinet maker, and in two years had saved enough money to return to school. Then good fortune came to the whole family. In 1830, Sarah Douglas married Julius Granger, a wealthy farmer from New York, and nine months later Mrs. Douglas married Gehazi Granger, the father of Julius. The whole family moved to the fine homestead of the Grangers in Canandaigua, New York.

Mr. Granger was kind and generous. Stephen was sent to a good school and finished his college preparatory work. But by this time he had decided to be a lawyer. Instead of going to college, he became a clerk in the office of the Hubbell brothers. Not only did Stephen learn good law here, but good manners as well. It was the custom of the partners each week to invite their clerks to dinner, to train them in the art of conversation and the niceties of social behavior.

From the time Stephen was a boy, Andrew Jackson had been his ideal, and life in the West his constant dream. When he was twenty, Stephen decided to adventure for himself in the West.

"When shall I see you again?" asked his mother on the day her son left home.

"I'll be back in ten years on my way to Congress," he replied confidently, for already he had chosen his career.

With the $300 he had saved, Stephen traveled until he reached Louisville, Kentucky. Then he decided to go to Jacksonville, Illinois, because it had been named in honor of Andrew Jackson.

But Jacksonville was a drab town with only a thousand people and eleven lawyers. There was no place here even for a clerk.

Next Stephen went to Winchester. Here he rented a one-room schoolhouse, secured forty pupils at three dollars each for the term, and taught for a year. He continued to read law, and at the end of the year, he returned to Jacksonville. He was given a license to practice law by the Illinois Supreme Court, for as yet the state did not require an examination. Stephen was not quite twenty-one years old then, but he wrote his mother that he was now "A Western man with Western feelings and principles."

Politics caught his interest from the beginning. There was a mid-term election that fall, but the Democrats had lost the county and there was much opposition to President Jackson.

"Let us have a meeting in the square and speak in defense of the President's policies," Stephen suggested to the Democrats.

On the day of the meeting, the square was

crowded. Stephen made such a fiery speech that the men swung him to their shoulders and paraded him around the town. "It's like David and Goliath!" they cried. "Douglas is a little giant."

"Little Giant!" It was to be his nickname for the rest of his life.

Not long after this, Douglas was appointed State's Attorney for Illinois. Abraham Lincoln, a new member in the legislature then meeting in Vandalia, caught his first glimpse of Douglas. "Why!" exclaimed Lincoln. "He's the least man I ever saw."

In 1837, the capital of Illinois was moved to Springfield. With the change of the capital, Lincoln, who had been most instrumental in bringing about that change, also moved to Springfield. And so did Douglas. From this time on, the lives of the two men began to intertwine.

Douglas had been made Register of the Land Office, a very fine position. He lived at the American House—the best hotel in Springfield. He dressed well, smoked expensive cigars, drank

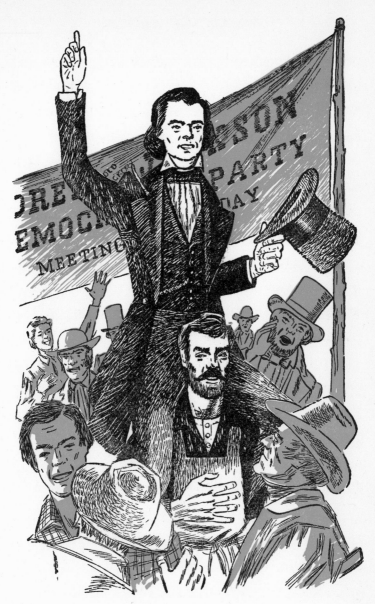

The men swung Douglas to their shoulders.

imported wine, and was invited everywhere. Although he was only five feet, four inches in height, Douglas was fine looking. His long brown hair was thick and curly; his features were strong; and his blue eyes had a merry twinkle. He was slim and quick and graceful. All of the women liked Douglas, but outside of his own family, politics was his only love.

In 1841, Douglas was made a Justice of the Supreme Court in Illinois. He was twenty-seven years old at the time and was the youngest man in the state ever to be given that position. But he was more interested in entering national politics. "What would you think," he wrote to his mother, "if Illinois would send your prodigal son to Congress?"

Then he told her how he secured votes. "I live with my constituents—eat, drink, lodge with them. Pray with them. Laugh, hunt, dance, and work with them. I eat their corn dodgers and fried bacon, and sleep two in a bed with them."

Douglas was elected to the House of Representatives in August, 1843. He traveled to Washington by way of New York so that his mother could see that his prediction had come true.

In the House that session, old John Quincy Adams was the leading figure. He had been the sixth President of the United States. But after his one term in office, Adams had been happy to be elected a representative from his own state of Massachusetts. He was to remain in that position until his death. Adams did not like the new representative from Illinois. He called Douglas a "dwarf" and a "pygmy." Perhaps, this was because in the House, Douglas made another enthusiastic speech about Jackson who was the longtime enemy of Adams.

Part of the time now, Douglas lived in Washington. In the House was David Reid, a young Democrat from North Carolina. In the spring of 1844, Douglas helped to entertain Reid's young cousin, Martha Martin. Later Douglas visited the Martins at their large plantation home in North Carolina, for he had fallen in love with Martha.

She was beautiful, well educated, and had a sweet disposition. They were married in April, 1847, shortly after Douglas was elected to the Senate.

On the day of the wedding, Mr. Martin offered his new son-in-law the deed to a Mississippi plantation worth $100,000. But Douglas refused the gift. So Colonel Martin left the property to his daughter, with the provision that if she died without children, the Negroes were to be freed. But in the will was this statement: "I would remind my dear daughter that her husband does not desire to own this kind of property." However, though Douglas did not own slaves himself, because of his marriage he had many friends who were Southerners, and so he understood and sympathized with their views.

When not in Washington, Senator and Mrs. Douglas lived in Chicago. In 1849, their first child, Robert, was born, and two years later a second boy, Stephen, whom they nicknamed "Steen." Douglas was devoted to his wife and children. Later Steen wrote of him, "I knew him as a boy may know his father—his friend, his playmate, and his chum, whom he loved and respected but never learned to fear."

Douglas was prosperous now. Martha had inherited a fortune, and her husband had a fine law practice and was making large sums in real estate. Douglas was like Chicago—full of energy, growing rapidly, amassing wealth, lavish and generous.

Then in 1853, Martha died. To soothe his grief, Douglas toured Europe for a year, leaving his boys in the care of his sister Sarah. In the fall of 1853, Douglas returned to the United States because he had a "cause" in mind. It was the building of a railroad to the Pacific. While in Europe, he had studied the transportation systems and had seen how trade was uniting Germany. A transcontinental railroad, he believed, would unite the teeming millions of the United States, and bring about an interchange of products that would make the whole nation prosperous.

Douglas wanted the railroad to start in Chicago

and go through Nebraska. He felt that Chicago had the greatest opportunity for growth in the Midwest. Furthermore, if the road were built, his real estate speculations would succeed. But the South wanted the railroad to start in Memphis, Tennessee, and go through New Mexico. The Southerners had an advantage in their choice of a route. New Mexico was organized as a territory, with a governor appointed by the President and confirmed by the Senate and a legislature elected by the people. Nebraska had no territorial government and was occupied by tribes of roaming Indians.

With the idea of getting the railroad built, Douglas originally proposed his Kansas-Nebraska Bill, for it would encourage settlement and thereby be a reason for building a railroad. But the Southern Congressmen fought the bill, and it could not be passed without their votes. Then an amendment to the bill was suggested to Douglas by Senator Dixon of Kentucky. This amendment would repeal the Missouri Compromise.

The Missouri Compromise had been passed in 1820. By its terms, all the land in the Louisiana Purchase Territory which was north of the line 36° 30', except the state of Missouri, would be "forever free." Both Kansas and Nebraska were in the territory north of the line. With the repeal of the law, it would be possible for those who moved into these areas to own slaves. If this happened, the Southerners would be satisfied and would end their opposition to the railroad line proposed by Douglas. They would vote for the Kansas-Nebraska Bill.

It was because of this amendment that the enemies of Douglas said he had proposed the bill not only to make money on his real estate speculations but to win the Democratic party's nomination for the presidency.

At this time, the Southern Democrats were not strong enough in numbers to have one of their own men nominated, but no candidate from the North could win the Democratic nomination without Southern support. Therefore, the author of a law which would make it possible for more territory to be open to slavery ought surely to win Southern votes.

All through January and February of 1854, Douglas, now with the help of the Southern Democrats, worked to have the Kansas-Nebraska Bill passed. By the first week of March, he was certain he could bring the matter to a vote. He must bring it to a vote. The thunder cloud of opposition was rushing through the political sky.

3. The Kansas-Nebraska Bill

THE YELLOW FLAMES OF THE GAS JETS IN THE chandeliers of the Senate Chamber flared high on the night of March 3, 1854, as a few weary visitors filed out of the gallery. It was nearly midnight, and the move to adjourn had just been defeated.

Shortly before, Douglas had asked for a vote on his Kansas-Nebraska Bill. But old Sam Houston, wearing his famous panther-skin vest with the skin side out, had stopped whittling his piece of soft pine wood and lumbered to his great height. "I move that we adjourn," he had bellowed.

There was a shout of, "No! No!" mostly from the Democrats.

"Then I'll speak on the bill," sputtered Houston.

"And I," shouted Senator Salmon P. Chase of Ohio who had led the opposition.

In grumpy silence, Sam Houston went back to his whittling, his big white hat pushed far back on his head. He had fought to make Texas a republic and had been its first president. Later when Texas had come into the Union, he had been elected Senator. But he was more familiar with bullets than with ballots, and so to ease his discomfort in debate, he whittled on small sticks of wood which the Senate pages brought to him.

As Sam Houston leaned back now on the back legs of his chair, with his feet up on his small lidded desk, the floor around him was piled high with shavings. For he feared secession, and his knife worked furiously as he heard Douglas beating down the opponents of a bill which would bring about the spread of slavery.

The Senate Chamber was jammed that night. It was a fine semicircular room with turkey-red carpet and a row of marble columns across the front. Most of the members were at their desks, but a few were gathered in front of the great hickory log fires at each end of the room. Some of the older men who were tired from the long debate of the day pulled heavy woolen shawls around their shoulders, and kept their hats on to shield their eyes from the glaring gaslights.

Stephen A. Douglas stood in the cleared space in front of the platform at which sat the presiding officer of the Senate. His dark blue eyes under their heavy eyebrows were intent with purpose. His strong chin was outthrust. His small right hand was raised to still the sullen murmurs of his opponents.

Like most of the senators who sat behind the small crowded desks, Douglas wore a black, loose-fitting frock coat, tight trousers, and a low-cut black satin vest showing an expanse of white starched shirt. His wing collar reached almost to his ears, and a black satin stock was wrapped around the collar and tied in a broad flat bow. The collar was wilted and the stock a trifle crooked now, for Douglas had been talking since noon. But no senator in that room could match his voice in strength and vibrancy, and none could beat him in debate.

Once more Douglas repeated the terms of the bill, and in his telling, it sounded so just and reasonable that his friends wondered why there should be argument against it.

It is true, said Douglas, that in the Missouri Compromise of 1820, the land in the Louisiana Purchase Territory north of the parallel 36° 30′ had been made "forever free." But in the Compromise of 1850, the territory which we had acquired from Mexico, except for California, was to be made into states in which there would be "no restrictions regarding slavery." Here the people could decide for themselves whether they wanted to be free or slave.

"This is 'popular sovereignty'—the right of

"It's the right of the people," cried Douglas.

the people to rule," cried Douglas, his voice filling every corner of the room, yet never seeming to shout. "It is a new idea for settling the slavery question, and it takes the place of the theory in the Missouri Compromise."

Therefore, he proposed that the Missouri Compromise be repealed, and that the Louisiana land north of 36° 30′ be divided into two territories to be called Kansas and Nebraska, wherein the *people* should have the right to decide whether they wanted their territory to be free or slave.

Throughout the debate and long after, Douglas insisted that he did not care whether slavery "was voted up or down" and that his only motive for the bill was "popular sovereignty," the right of the people to rule.

As we read about the various motives that Douglas might have had for proposing the bill, it is hard to determine which was his real reason. Many historians have disagreed on this point, but many of them have been prejudiced for or against Douglas.

Most of the arguments of Douglas were directed against the leaders of the opposition, Senator Chase of Ohio and Senator Sumner of Massachusetts who were Abolitionists, and Senator Seward of New York who was the leader of the Whigs.

"The Missouri Compromise is a sacred pledge

to which the Democrats of the South agreed," argued Senator Sumner.

"It has been set aside by the Compromise of 1850," Douglas stubbornly insisted.

Then Senator Seward made a speech to show that the bill would keep poor white settlers from moving to the West. "A man who has only his two hands and a few small tools cannot compete with a wealthy Southern slave owner," was his argument.

"Geographical conditions will keep the Southern planter from Nebraska," answered Douglas. "This bill will organize two territories. Let the South have Kansas, and let the North have Nebraska. Then both sides will be satisfied."

Senator Chase then renewed his personal attacks on Douglas. He was sponsoring the bill to win the presidency and to make a fortune in real estate, accused Chase.

But the three men together were no match for Stephen A. Douglas. He was like a Roman gladiator, pulling up his shield of defense or thrusting

AREA AFFECTED BY
KANSAS-NEBRASKA BILL

out his sword with short, swift words of attack.
He was determined that the vote should be taken
before the Senate adjourned for the day.

Until this week, Douglas had been sure of the
passage of his bill. He knew that nearly all the
Southern senators would vote for it and many
Northern senators as well. Not only in New Eng-

48

land but all through the North, until recently, people had not felt strongly enough against slavery to want to run the risk of having the Southern states withdraw from the Union.

But ever since the Kansas-Nebraska Bill had been amended, the hostility in the North toward slavery had been on the increase. Daily the ranks of the Abolitionists grew, and in far-off Wisconsin there was talk of a new political party that had started, a party made up of men who were disgusted with the weak leadership of the Whigs and the Democrats.

And Senator Douglas knew this. With the passing of each day, Northern senators who had been on his side might be won over to the opposition. There must be a vote on the bill before another day went by.

One o'clock. Two o'clock. Three o'clock in the morning. On went the debate. Sumner, Chase and Seward were furious but helpless.

"The only power that can destroy slavery immediately is the sword," cried Douglas at last.

49

"It will die out eventually, of that I am sure. But I am not willing to set fire to the ship to smoke out the rats." It was his most telling argument. There were few in that room who wanted to "set fire to the ship."

Finally the roll was called. The bill was passed by a vote of 37 to 14. Only two Southerners, Sam Houston a Democrat, and John Bell of Tennessee, a Whig, voted against it. A pale gray light filtered through the curtains of the tall windows of the Senate Chamber. At five o'clock the presiding officer pounded his gavel for adjournment.

Down the steps of the Capitol and out into the cold bitter dawn went the weary lawmakers. Sleepy drivers pulled up their lamp-lighted coaches. A horsedrawn omnibus paused at the foot of the hill to take on passengers. Some of the men strode briskly down Pennsylvania Avenue, pulling tight their heavy capes or woolen shawls.

Chase and Sumner were among the last to

leave. They were devoted friends, but the bitterness of defeat was like unripe fruit in their mouths. From the Navy Yard came the boom of cannon shots announcing the passage of the bill.

"They celebrate a present victory," said Chase gloomily. "But the echoes will never rest until slavery itself shall die."

Sumner nodded. He was remembering what Chase had said in one of his speeches against the bill. "This bill will light up a fire in the country that may consume in the end those who have kindled it."

What would happen to Douglas? What would happen to the Democratic party? What would happen to the nation?

4. The Birth of the Republican Party

ALL OVER NEW ENGLAND AND IN THE EASTERN states mass meetings, much like the one that has been described, had been called during the early months of 1854 to protest the Kansas-Nebraska Bill. Douglas had been called "Arnold" rather than "Stephen" Douglas. Someone sent him thirty pieces of silver and named him "Judas." He was to see figures of himself stuffed with straw, doused with oil, and set on fire until he said he could "travel from Boston to Chicago" in the light of his own effigies.

But at none of the meetings had there been much thought of starting a new political organization to stop the spread of slavery. The Whigs and the Democrats were too strong, or their leaders were too anxious to preserve their prestige, for anyone of influence to break away from one of the old parties because of a single issue. It was in the little far-off village of Ripon, Wisconsin, that a handful of eager and earnest men had the courage to make that break.

Ripon at that time was a newly formed frontier settlement with less than five hundred people. One of its early settlers was Major Alvan Bovay. He was a lawyer and one-time teacher of languages who had served in the Mexican War and had moved to Ripon from New Jersey.

The Major was like a steam engine without a safety valve whenever he thought of the Kansas-Nebraska Bill. He was disgusted with the fearful Northern leaders of the Democratic and Whig parties who, even though they were opposed to slavery, were so afraid of secession that they would do nothing to anger the South.

"The only way we'll prevent the spread of

slavery," said the Major to anyone who would listen to him, "is to organize a new party which will include all those opposed to slavery."

On February 28, 1854, there appeared an advertisement in the *Ripon Herald*, the weekly newspaper of the town. There would be a meeting at six-thirty, the following Wednesday evening in the Congregational Church. All those who wanted to "remonstrate against the Nebraska swindle" were invited to attend. At the meeting, a resolution was passed to start a new party to prevent the spread of slavery in the event the Kansas-Nebraska Bill became a law.

When the bill passed the Senate on March 4th, another meeting was called for March 20th, this time in the little one-room schoolhouse. It was a cold, windy night. The candles on the teacher's desk where Major Bovay presided and on the long knife-grooved desks of the pupils burned low, and some guttered out as the meeting proceeded. But before the group went home, a new party had been formed. The citizens had gone into the schoolhouse as Whigs, Democrats, Free-Soilers and Abolitionists. They came out as members of a new party which they thought should be called "Republican."

Major Bovay was a close friend of Horace Greeley, the famous editor of *The New York Tribune*. To him the Major wrote several letters regarding the name of the party. "A good name is a tower of strength," he wrote. "Democracy is a word which charms, and Republican is its only counterpart."

The Major was making a good choice. A democracy is a form of government in which everyone has a share and in which the will of the citizens prevails. Therefore, "Democratic" party meant that this was the party of the people. However, a country like England which is ruled by a monarch is a democracy because the ruler has very limited powers, and the country is really controlled by the House of Commons in Parliament which is elected by the people.

A republic is a form of government, such as

the United States, in which the people select not only the lawmaking body but all the agents who run their country. Therefore, a republic is the most democratic form of representative government. That is why Major Bovay said that the name "Republican" for his new party would be the only "counterpart" for "Democratic."

Major Bovay wanted his friend Horace Greeley to declare himself in favor of the new party. But Greeley was reluctant at this time to be identified with it. He was an important leader of the Whigs in New York. If he abandoned his own well-established party and joined up with this weak and at present unimportant organization, he might lose all his influence. He was not ready to make such a sacrifice.

Meetings like those in Ripon were held in other parts of the country. In Strong, Maine, and in Friendship, New York, there are records of similar organizations though later than the one at Ripon. By the time the New York meeting was held in May, 1854, Editor Greeley was more

The audience sat or stood under the wide-spreading trees.

positive in his views. When questioned this time in a letter from a local editor regarding a party name, Greeley replied, "Call it Republican—no prefix, no suffix, just plain Republican." This is why Greeley later claimed the credit for christening the new party.

The Kansas-Nebraska Bill was passed in the House on May 22nd and signed by the President on May 30th. But from the time of its passage in the Senate, there were appeals in newspapers all over the North for "honest men to get together and rebuke the violated pledges of the South."

Most historians consider July 6, 1854, at Jackson, Michigan, as the official birthday and birthplace of the Republican Party. Although the name had been used during the year for local political groups, this was the first time a formal convention was called, at which a platform was adopted and candidates named.

As soon as the Kansas-Nebraska Bill became a law, a group of leading citizens in Detroit issued a call for a mass meeting to be held in Jackson at one o'clock on Thursday, July 6, 1854. Here plans would be made "for a union at the North to protect liberty from being overthrown."

Delegations from all over the state began to arrive on Wednesday, coming by special train, wagon and horseback. By nine o'clock on Thursday morning, there were three thousand strangers in Jackson and as many more home people. As no hall was large enough to hold this crowd, the meeting was adjourned to a grove of stately oak trees on land belonging to Elisha Morgan just outside of the town.

It was a beautiful day, bright but not too warm. A rough platform and some seats had been erected on a grassy mound for the speakers and officials, while the audience sat or stood under the wide-spreading trees. Before the day was over, most of those present, much to the dismay of Mr. Morgan, had hacked off a strip of an oak for a souvenir, for they realized they were making history, though how much no one guessed.

The meeting began promptly. Those in charge

had made careful plans. Various committees adjourned down the road, and it was not long before a platform had been adopted, candidates nominated, and the name "Republican" chosen for the party.

The nominating committee made every effort as they had been instructed to name "tried, true, and honest men whom the people will trust." All other anti-slavery groups present promised to support the candidates for the new party. As a result, at the election in November, 1854, the Republicans had a sweeping victory in Michigan, so that it became the first Republican state.

Few of the bankers, or manufacturers, or merchants, or political leaders, or other men of property or high position in the North worked to organize the opposition to the spread of slavery. Instead, those who lived in the back streets of the manufacturing towns, or on small outlying farms, or in little communities, and the editors of their weekly newspapers were the leaders. For it was the humble, less significant people whose feelings seemed most aroused and who had the courage and the determination to act.

In Boston, only the poets and other literary people who were idealistic and who had the courage to fight for a cause joined the ranks of this new movement. The people with capital still worked in their own well-organized parties to do nothing that would antagonize the South. They wanted to continue their profitable business relations with the South, and they were afraid that continued Northern hostility would make the South secede.

This may be hard to understand, for apparently the North had every advantage in Congress. There were 147 representatives in Congress from the North and only 90 from the South.

Then why did the wishes of the South dominate?

First of all, even though the North had more people, only a small proportion of them were Abolitionists. The rest were either lukewarm or indifferent in their feeling against slavery. In the South, almost everyone favored slavery.

As a rule, the Southern Congressmen were men of wealth, education and social position. They had a dash and vigor that the Northern men lacked, and they swept the imagination. No wonder they were called "fire eaters." Added to this, was the leadership in the Democratic party of Stephen A. Douglas, a Northern man but with Southern sympathies, and the best debater of them all. It was not until 1858, when Douglas was drawn into debate with Lincoln, that he met his match.

Yet had Douglas foreseen that he might light the spark that would start a great political conflagration, he probably never would have sponsored the Kansas-Nebraska Bill. Douglas loved the Union and was devoted to the Democratic party. He would have done nothing knowingly to injure either one.

But in spite of his many fine qualities, Douglas lacked insight and caution. Success had spoiled him. Rarely had a man reached such a high political position at such an early age. This made him overconfident, so that he made decisions quickly and did not follow through in his thinking to determine what would be the results.

In spite of his Kansas-Nebraska bill, Douglas did not believe that slavery would be extended. He thought that climate and other natural conditions would make it unprofitable for a slaveholder to move into the new territory. To him, the bill was a gesture to please the South and in this way end the opposition to his proposed railroad line. So Douglas and the men who followed him paid little attention at first to this new and struggling political organization.

Even the statesmen who were strongly opposed to slavery were reluctant to join the new party. In the beginning Chase, Seward, Sumner, and Thurlow Weed, the "boss" of the Whig party, did little to help the Republican cause. Editor Greeley, although he worked hard against the Kansas-Nebraska Bill, did not display the Republican

William Lloyd Garrison edited The Liberator.

banner on his newspaper until the party was well established.

We can understand this better if we learn about the other political parties opposed to slavery which had developed before this time. There were several, but none had any great strength. The Free-Soilers were an anti-slavery group who were willing to permit slavery where it already existed but were opposed to its spread. More radical were the Abolitionists. They considered slaveholding a sin and wanted immediate freedom for the slaves with no payment for the owners. Their leader, William Lloyd Garrison, was the editor of *The Liberator*, an extreme anti-slavery newspaper.

The most important of the minor groups was the American Party, more familiarly called the "Know Nothings." It was a secret society to which only Protestants who were not married to Catholics were admitted. It had been formed to stop the flood of immigration of Germans and Irish to this country. Whenever members of the party were questioned, they were bound by oath to answer, "I know nothing." It was for this reason that Greeley called them the "Know Nothings." Later because members of the party also were opposed to the spread of slavery, they joined the Republicans.

But none of these minor parties had been able to displace the Whigs or the Democrats, and their leaders had little influence. So why should men who had been long in political life think that this new anti-slavery group would become important?

Only in the Midwest did the party have any great strength from the beginning. Here the states were close to the ones into which slavery might spread. In the Midwest, the political leaders were young men and less hidebound by political tradition. The old party organizations were not as strong as in the East, and so it was less difficult for men with new ideas to throw off the shackles of the Whigs and the Democrats.

Perhaps, after all, the time was ripe for a new political party. Although the Kansas-Nebraska Bill had ignited the political flame, there were other contributing causes.

The Whigs and the Democrats, in their anxiety to appease everybody and thereby maintain unity, had become politically stagnant. The time in history was a time of movement and social reform, not only in this country but in England. Prisons and workhouses had been improved; more people had been given the right to vote; and temperance societies had started. It was natural that men in this country should think about the inhumanity of slavery. Political leaders who were in line with the times and who would wish to foster new ideas were the ones who would achieve the greatest influence.

Although the Abolitionists were small in number, they were loud and unceasing in their denunciation of slavery. "I will be as harsh as truth and as uncompromising as justice—and I will be heard," said Garrison. His ideas might be radical, but they served to arouse the people who heard him to take a less extreme course—at least to organize to prevent the spread of slavery.

5. The Tall Giant from Illinois

ABRAHAM LINCOLN HAD BEEN ONE OF THE Whig leaders in Illinois who had been reluctant to join the new party. It was only when he realized that the Whigs would do nothing to stop the spread of slavery that he decided to become "unwhigged" as he described it to a friend. For Lincoln to make that decision was most important, for in 1856 he was a political leader in his state.

It had not always been so. In March, 1837, with seven dollars in cash in his pocket and a one thousand dollar debt to be paid, Lincoln had ridden on a borrowed horse from New Salem to Springfield. He was twenty-eight years old

68

then, but he had a license to practice law. John T. Stuart, one of the best lawyers in Illinois, had offered him a partnership.

It was Stuart who had convinced Lincoln that lack of a formal education was no handicap to becoming a lawyer and had loaned him books. It had been hard work for Lincoln to read and memorize the books while working in New Salem. He had served no apprenticeship in a law office, and had taught himself how to write wills, deeds and other legal papers from a book of forms.

But he had taken part in politics ever since he had cast his first vote. He was in his second term in the legislature in 1837, the year he came to Springfield, and had worked the hardest to have the capital moved to that town. So why shouldn't the new capital be a place of golden opportunity for him?

In Springfield, a young man, Joshua Speed, asked Lincoln to share with him the sleeping quarters in the large attic room over Speed's general merchandise store. William Herndon, who later became Lincoln's law partner, but who was clerking for Speed at the time, also slept in the attic room. The three men became very good companions.

Speed had come from a well-to-do family in Kentucky before starting his business in Springfield. He was Lincoln's closest friend during these first years. Even after Speed returned to Kentucky to start a new home with his young bride, the two men wrote long and intimate letters to each other. It is from a study of these letters that one gets the most revealing details in Lincoln's life and manner of thinking.

Having secured a place to sleep, the new lawyer next went to Stuart's office overlooking the square and hung up his shingle. "Abraham Lincoln, Attorney and Counsellor at Law," he wrote on the fly leaf of his dictionary to see how it would look. Then he went out to get business, make friends and build his political fences.

The heart of Springfield was around the square where the new Capitol was to be built. Near the square, in a big two-story brick house with porches on the side and plenty of scrollwork for decoration, lived Ninian W. Edwards, the leader of Springfield aristocracy. His father had been the first senator from Illinois and one of its early governors. Ninian had married Elizabeth Todd, whose family were wealthy and influential in Lexington, Kentucky.

In 1839 Elizabeth's sister Mary had come to Springfield to pay a long visit. Many young girls seeking husbands came to Springfield. There were ten men to every woman, for not only did the legislature meet there, but the court sessions were held in the capital. Throughout the long winter, the hospitable citizenry provided entertainment for the visitors.

Through Joshua Speed, Lincoln was made welcome to the parties, though his social progress was slow. But in December, 1839, Lincoln with several other young men was a "manager" for a social gathering known as a "cotillion" to be

71

given at the Edwards' mansion to celebrate the opening of the legislature.

Candles bloomed like yellow crocuses in double rows on both sashes of all the windows in the Edwards' big brick house. Carriages rolled up the circular driveway, and young men tied their horses to the ornamental posts at the edge of the lawn. Lincoln came late. He felt clumsy in his poorly fitting black frock coat and heavy boots, and he had little grace in dancing except in a few figures of the square dances.

For a while, Lincoln stood watching in the doorway of the parlor. The small, tufted chairs had been pushed against the walls, and the glow from the candles in the crystal chandeliers made pools of light in the dark polished floor.

Then Abraham Lincoln saw Mary Todd. She was small and rather plump, though this was not so apparent in her style of dress. The Swiss embroidered ruffles of her wide-skirted dress had been brought from New Orleans by her father. She wore a garland of roses in her light brown

Lincoln almost lifted Mary in the air when he danced.

hair, and more tiny roses were in the knots of ribbon which tied her short gloves.

Mary's face was round and dimpled, with a straight nose and short upper lip. Her clear blue eyes sparkled with laughter. In and out from under her billowing skirts, darted her small pink satin slippers. "Mary was like a spray of pink and white apple blossoms dancing lightly in the breeze," her niece once wrote of her.

Stephen Douglas was her partner in the polka they were dancing, for he had come early, as was proper, and lined up with the other managers to receive the guests. When the music ended, Joshua Speed presented his friend. "Miss Todd, I want to dance with you in the worst way," said Lincoln.

And "worst" it was, for he stepped all over her pretty satin slippers and almost lifted her from the floor with his long arms when he "polked."

Throughout that year and the next, Lincoln courted Mary Todd. He called her by her nickname "Molly" and wrote to her father, Robert

Todd, asking permission to marry his daughter. Lincoln was a lonely, lovesick young man with little knowledge or acquaintanceship with women, and Mary held him entranced.

But Lincoln was not Mary's only suitor. There was a widower, Edwin Webb, sixteen years older than Mary and with two children. Douglas also called on her frequently, but he was too devoted to his own family and too interested in politics to think of matrimony.

Once Mrs. Edwards asked Mary which man she would marry.

"The one who has the best chance to become President," answered Mary. But that probably was a young girl's hope for a wonderful future.

The courtship of Lincoln was not encouraged by the Edwardses. He was not sufficiently educated, said Elizabeth, "to hold a conversation with a lady." He differed in nature, mind and raising from her sister.

"I would rather marry a good man of mind with bright prospects ahead for position than to marry all the houses and gold in the world," said Mary, with a dig for her sister who had married with the "houses and gold" in mind.

Mary seemed to have everything that Lincoln wanted in a wife. She had good looks, feminine ways and polished manners. To a lonely, awkward man like Lincoln, slow in showing his emotions and with moods of deep depression, Mary was a shining light, for she was generous, loving and demonstrative. He overlooked her willfulness, her quick temper, and her sharp wit, or thought them only girlish faults which would be quickly changed with womanhood and a husband's firm control.

Toward the end of 1840, Lincoln and Mary were engaged, and there were elaborate plans for a wedding. There are conflicting stories after this, but in the beginning of 1841 the engagement was broken. For months, Lincoln had spells of melancholy, for he missed the brightness of his courtship. Then he and Mary were brought together by a friend.

Once more plans were made for a wedding. Because of all that had happened, Mary had decided not to tell her family. On the morning of his wedding day, Lincoln met Ninian Edwards in the square and told him of the wedding plans.

"Mary is my ward and must be married in my house," insisted Ninian.

The big house was hurriedly made ready, attendants secured and a supper prepared. The ceremony took place in front of the fireplace in the parlor, while rain poured steadily down the tall, narrow windows of the room. The groom was thirty-three and his bride ten years younger. He had bought her a gold wedding ring with "Love is Eternal" inscribed on the inside.

There were years of hardship at first for the Lincolns. They lived in a boarding house for a time. Then in 1844, they bought the house on Eighth and Jackson Streets in which they lived for the rest of their years in Springfield.

In 1841, Lincoln had dissolved his partnership with Stuart and had become the partner of

Stephen T. Logan. It was in this office that Lincoln learned to study cases carefully until he became a capable, all-round lawyer, and one of the best jury lawyers in Illinois.

He was known as Honest Abe now and also Old Abe though he was in his early thirties. But loneliness and privation had made deep furrows on the barren field of his long bony face. People knew him as quick and strong though awkward in his movements. They knew him as ambitious, eager to learn, hard to deceive, and the best stump speaker in the state.

Everybody quoted his apt and humorous stories. All he would have to do when eating at a table was to put his knife and fork down, lean forward on his elbows and say, "That reminds me," and immediately the faces of his listeners would begin to twitch in expectation of the droll story that was coming.

"He could make a cat laugh," they said, but there were times when his face was the saddest and loneliest in all the world.

The Lincolns had four children: Robert, Eddie, Willie and Thomas, who was nicknamed Tad. At least half of each year, Lincoln spent riding circuit. He enjoyed this in spite of the hardships of travel, but it left his family very lonely. In 1844, Lincoln decided to have his own law office, and asked William Herndon, then a law student in Logan's office, to be his partner.

Herndon was a fine looking man of medium height, about ten years younger than Lincoln. The two men were unlike in many ways. Herndon was a heavy drinker and had most of the vices of the time. He had little political ambition. Lincoln neither drank, smoked nor even chewed tobacco; and politics was his breath and life.

In spite of their differences, Herndon idolized the older man and was a loyal and devoted friend. There was absolute honesty in their business relations. They divided all fees equally without question and without receipts, no matter who deserved the larger share.

In 1846, Lincoln was elected to the United

States House of Representatives. He was not a candidate for re-election. After this, he applied for the position of United States Land Commissioner but was refused. He was offered the governorship of the Territory of Oregon, but declined this because Mary objected to going so far west to live. For the next five years he devoted himself to building up his law practice.

Then came the passage of the Kansas-Nebraska Bill. "I was losing interest in politics when the repeal of the Missouri Compromise aroused me again," Lincoln wrote to a friend. For although he thought the Abolitionists too radical, he was opposed to the spread of slavery. He had learned of the horrors of slavery when he had journeyed down the Mississippi River on a flatboat to New Orleans and there had his first sight of a slave auction block. During the two years he had been in Congress, he had watched the slave market from the very windows of the Capitol.

Now. though he was reluctant to leave the

There he had his first sight of a slave auction block.

Whig party, he realized that the Republican party must become united in the North if the spread of slavery was to stop. The organization of the party had been slow in Illinois. The sentiment in the state regarding slavery was sharply divided. The northern portion was anti-slavery, but in the southern part of the state lived many families who had come from the South and whose forefathers had been slaveholders. These people naturally supported Douglas and the Kansas-Nebraska Bill.

Finally, in May, 1856, the Republicans in Illinois met in Bloomington to form a state party and to choose delegates for the forthcoming national convention. Abraham Lincoln was one of the most prominent speakers at the meeting. From that time on, the history of the whole Republican party revolved more and more around this political leader from Illinois.

6. *And So the Party Grew*

THE FIRST NATIONAL REPUBLICAN CONVEN-
tion to nominate a candidate for President was
held in Philadelphia, in June, 1856. By this time,
Seward, Chase and Sumner had joined the party.
But under the leadership of Thurlow Weed, for-
merly the "boss" of the Whig party, the convention by-passed these leaders. They were considered too radical in their opposition to slavery.
As yet, the various groups in the Republican
party were held together only by their desire to
prevent the extension of slavery and to bring
about the repeal of the Kansas-Nebraska Law.
Anyone who favored the complete abolition of
slavery would still have too small a following to

win many votes in a nation-wide contest like the presidential election.

John C. Fremont was nominated for the presidency by the Republicans although he was comparatively unknown in politics. He had been born in Georgia and was of French descent. But even though he had been a Southern Democrat, he was strongly opposed to slavery. Perhaps this was because he had lived out of the South during most of his adult life. He was forty-three years old at the time he was nominated, but since early manhood his name had been associated with romance and high adventure.

When Fremont was twenty-eight, he had eloped with Jessie Benton, the beautiful sixteen-year-old daughter of Senator Thomas Benton of Missouri. As an army engineer, Fremont had explored the Rocky Mountains and had won the nickname of "Pathfinder." During the Mexican War, he had overthrown the Mexican government in California and had been made military governor and later elected senator from California. He was an heroic and colorful personality who captured the imagination of the idealists in the Republican party. But he was not a good political leader.

Abraham Lincoln was one of the candidates for the vice-presidency, but was defeated by William L. Dayton of New Jersey. However, Lincoln worked vigorously throughout the campaign, for not only did he believe in the cause, but politics once again had captured his interest.

The Democrats chose James Buchanan of Pennsylvania, a Northern man but with Southern sympathies, for their presidential candidate. Former President Millard Fillmore was nominated by the Know Nothings.

The Whig party named no candidate in 1856. By this time, most of the Northern Whigs had become Republicans, while the Southern Whigs had joined forces with the Democratic party.

The rallying cry of the Republicans in 1856 was, "Free speech, free press, free labor, and Fremont!" For the most part, the men who campaigned the hardest were not politicians or office seekers, in spite of the fact that the political leaders of the North had now joined the party. In New England, especially, the Republicans were led by men of literature and of the church.

By this time, the opposition of Northern clergymen to slavery had become so intense that the Presbyterian and Methodist churches had split into Northern and Southern branches. Although the Democrats protested that clergymen should confine their political activities to casting a vote, the ministers in the Northern churches felt they had the right to speak from their pulpits whenever the issue was moral and humanitarian as well as political. On the Sunday before election day, public prayers for the success of Fremont were said in many of the Northern churches.

The New England writers like Emerson, Thoreau, Whittier and Longfellow begged votes for Fremont. Longfellow in a letter to Senator Sumner stated that the one reason he was not going to Europe that summer was because he did not want to lose his vote. "I have great respect for that now," he wrote. "Though I never cared about it before."

But the South again threatened secession if Fremont were elected. Buchanan promised a fair vote in Kansas if he would win. The right of a people to decide on their own way of life as proposed in the Kansas-Nebraska Law seemed to many people the most democratic way to settle the slavery question. And Fremont did not display strong leadership. For these reasons, Buchanan was elected. But, although he won the electoral vote, his popular vote was 400,000 less than the combined votes of his opponents.

From the standpoint of history, it was fortunate that Fremont was defeated. The South might have been successful in forming a new government in 1856. The North was neither united enough in anti-slavery sentiment nor strong enough in manpower and production to prevent secession at that time. Buchanan promised a fair deal in Kansas. The country quietly waited to see if this would happen. For a time it seemed that the Republican party, like other anti-slavery organizations, would be remembered only in the pages of the history books.

Then two days after the inauguration of Buchanan, the United States Supreme Court gave a decision which tore the nation apart as much as had the Kansas-Nebraska Bill.

At noon on Friday, March 6, 1857, led by Chief Justice Roger B. Taney, the nine justices of the Supreme Court in their rustling black silk robes walked slowly to their high-backed chairs on the platform in the Supreme Court Chamber. It was a rather small room on the ground floor of the Capitol, and that day it was packed with spectators. Behind the judges was the oil painting of former Chief Justice John Marshall. Facing them was a marble plaque of the scales of justice. There were many who would think that the anti-slavery scale wavered downward that day.

88

Rarely has our Supreme Court had a membership held in greater respect than at that time. The justices were all men of high character and ability. Four of them were from the North and five from the South. All but two were Democrats. But not even the Southern justices were slaveholders, and all of the men were devoted to the Constitution and the Union.

Roger B. Taney of Virginia had been appointed by President Jackson on the death of John B. Marshall. In Taney's twenty-two years on the bench, he had won the respect and affection of the whole nation. He was well educated and was a wide reader. He was a devout Catholic, and it was his custom to kneel down in prayer for a few minutes before going to the bench. There is no doubt that his prayers must have been especially fervent that chill morning in early March.

There was almost pin-drop silence in the chamber as the spectators waited for Taney to speak. He was tall and gaunt with sallow skin, large features and a wide mouth. His gray hair fell in slight disorder on his high forehead; and as he spoke, he occasionally brushed it back with his large bony hand. The deep furrows on his face were etched with grief today, for his wife and daughter had died the previous year of yellow fever and until recently he had been broken in health by his loss. He was almost eighty years old, but in spite of his years and his grief, no one questioned Taney's ability to give a just and intelligent decision.

The case before the Court that morning was that of Dred Scott of Missouri versus John Sanford of New York. Dred Scott was a Negro slave who had belonged to an army surgeon, Dr. John Emerson of St. Louis. In 1834, the doctor had taken Scott from St. Louis to an army post in Illinois and then to one in Wisconsin. Slavery was prohibited in both. In 1838, Dr. Emerson had returned to St. Louis, bringing Scott with him. At the time Scott had made no protest regarding his continued enslavement.

But in 1846, after the death of Dr. Emerson,

Scott sued Mrs. Emerson for his freedom on the
ground that he had been taken into free territory.
It is thought that Abolitionist leaders rather than
Scott were back of the case, for a long time had
passed and the Negro was an uneducated man.

The case went through the various courts in
Missouri and then into the United States Circuit
Court when Scott was sold to John Sanford of
New York. In each court, Scott's plea for freedom was denied for the reason that as a Negro
he was not a citizen and had no right to bring his
case to court. Judge Taney was to announce this
day whether the lower courts had been right in
their decisions.

"The Negro," read Judge Taney in his low,
hollow voice, "is so far inferior to the white man
that he could not sue in the court as a citizen and
so is still a slave." There were restrained movements among the spectators in the chamber. This
was the expected decision.

Judge Taney might have rested his case there
since his decision was the same as the lower courts.

But to the decision he now added an "opinion" regarding the Missouri Compromise. He argued that the right of property in slaves was expressly stated in the Constitution, and therefore Congress had no more right to make laws regarding slavery than over any other property. The Missouri Com-

The judge read the decision in the Dred Scott case.

People gathered to discuss the court decision.

promise, therefore, was *unconstitutional and void*. It was the opinion and not the decision that aroused the nation.

Six of the justices agreed with Taney. Only the two Republicans dissented. According to the Republicans, Negroes had the right to vote in five of the original thirteen states at the time the Constitution was written. Therefore, they were not considered "inferior" to the white man. Furthermore, there had been eight cases including the Missouri Compromise in which Congress had excluded slavery in the territories, and these laws had been signed by seven Presidents.

In justice to the members of the Court, it must be repeated that they were all men of learning and honesty. But the seven who were Democrats mingled on close social terms with the important leaders of the South. Furthermore, both Congress and the administration were dominated by Southerners. It was natural that the justices would be influenced by their views. They had been persuaded that if the Supreme Court made a decision favorable to slavery, sectional hatred would end and civil war would be avoided.

Rarely has a Supreme Court decision aroused so much feeling. The reaction was completely sectional. The Southerners hailed it as a rebuke to the Abolitionists. The Northerners said they would not obey it. "The Supreme Court," shouted the Northern newspapers, had "dragged its garments in the filth of pro-slavery politics." As a consequence, more and more people joined the Republican party. Not long after the decision, Dred Scott and his family were bought by a Republican member of Congress who freed all of them.

And so the party grew. With the mid-term election in 1858, the strength of the Republicans showed decided increase. In the Congressional elections which were held, all of the free states except Illinois and California had Republican victories. Slowly but surely the North was uniting against the further spread of slavery.

7. *"Bleeding Kansas"*

In THE MEANTIME, THE HISTORY OF KANSAS AS a territory had begun, but many of the pages were to be written in blood. Immediately after the passage of the Kansas-Nebraska Bill, pro-slavery families from Missouri which was a slave state began moving into Kansas. Since 1849, there had been no land which was free for settlement, and people who lived near the border of Kansas had been waiting impatiently for the opening of this new territory. There was little immigration by the Missourians into Nebraska, for there was no expectation of making it into a slave state.

Some of the families came by steamboat along the rivers. Others traveled in caravans of canvas-topped wagons with "Kansas" painted crudely on the gray-white covers. The men wore red flannel shirts, buckskin trousers, and heavy boots, and were armed with guns and bowie knives. No

Some traveled in caravans of canvas-topped wagons.

one person was in authority, and all shared the hardships of the journey. The settlers from Missouri were determined that their votes should make Kansas a slaveholding state, but they also wanted to make a home in this fertile new country.

But the Missourians were not the only immigrants. In New England, Eli Thayer started the Emigrant Aid Company. Its purpose was to send Free Soil settlers to Kansas, and to provide them with land, equipment, and supplies. The settlers were equally determined that Kansas should be a free state. Later, with their picks and shovels, they brought along the newly invented Sharps rifles, for they expected to have to fight for their land.

Once Henry Ward Beecher, the famous pastor of the Plymouth Church in Brooklyn and brother of Harriet Beecher Stowe, sent the settlers a box with twenty-five Bibles and the same number of Sharps rifles. The box was labeled "Bibles," so that from that day on Sharps rifles were nick-named "Beecher's Bibles."

The free-state men founded the town of Lawrence while the chief settlement of the pro-slavery men was Lecompton. It was not long before the expected fighting started. "Free state or slave state?" was the greeting as men moved toward each other with rifles or pistols ready to fire. But there was little organized resistance. The conflicts which occurred were more like the mountain feuds of a later day, and any settler's log cabin could become a fortified position.

In March, 1855, Andrew Reeder, who had been appointed governor, called for an election of members to a territorial legislature. At this time, the pro-slavery settlers far outnumbered those from the free states. But to make sure of winning, on election day, 5,000 Missourians crossed the border and voted for pro-slavery representatives.

There was no pretense at legality. Whole communities of men on horseback or driving wagons loaded with provisions crossed the rivers and camped near the towns in Kansas the night before the election. Some voters went through the form of driving a stake or nailing a card with their name to a tree as if they were going to claim land. If judges of the election protested because the men were not registered voters, pro-slavery judges were put in their places. As a result, the pro-slavery group had an overwhelming victory.

But the invasion was a big mistake for the Missourians. In the census that year, about 3,000 voters had been registered. On election day, more than 6,000 votes were cast. From that day on, all the Missourians were labeled "border ruffians," and the Republicans had a real cause for protest.

The free-state men completely disregarded the result of the election. Instead, they met in Topeka in October, 1855, and elected their own men to a constitutional convention. A constitution was drawn up declaring Kansas a free state, and it was submitted to Congress for approval. It passed in the House where, because of greater population, there were more representatives from the North, but it was rejected in the Senate.

From then on, Kansas continued with two communities living in separate towns and governed by separate laws. Guerrilla bands roamed the territory. The fields were neglected unless

Pro-slavery men set fire to the hotel and looted the town.

cared for by the women and children. When men tried to harvest their crops, they worked in groups and were fully armed.

In May, 1856, the pro-slavery men attacked the free town of Lawrence. They burned the newspaper presses, set fire to the new hotel, and looted the town, though no lives were lost. In revenge, John Brown and his four sons went at night into a pro-slavery settlement and brutally murdered five men.

John Brown was a New Englander of Puritan descent. He was an upright and honest man who was sincerely religious but intolerant. He believed without question the statements that were made in the Bible. "Fear God and keep His commandments," was the rule by which John Brown lived. He had a large family who were completely controlled by their father, so that he was always able to get help for any of his undertakings.

Because of his strong personality, commanding presence and deep convictions, Brown also was able to get financial help from wealthy men who shared his views. For years he had brooded over the evils of slavery. Finally he became convinced he was ordained by God to free the slaves. He had come to Kansas with his sons to join in the fight to make it a free state. "It has been decreed by God," said John Brown whenever there was any argument regarding his course of conduct.

John Brown felt no guilt over the murder of the five men. "God is my judge," said he. "The people of Kansas will justify my course." He was right. Although at first, the free-state men were horrified by the deed, there was no punishment for the crime.

Shortly after the first territorial election in Kansas, Governor Reeder was dismissed by President Pierce apparently for being too sympathetic with the free-state settlers. In turn, three other governors were appointed but had little more success than Reeder in establishing order. At last, federal troops were sent and a form of government was maintained. Later an estimate was made of the amount of damage. About two million dollars in livestock, crops and buildings had been destroyed, and 200 lives had been lost.

Ignoring what had been done by the free-state convention in Topeka, the pro-slavery legislature drew up a constitution at Lecompton and submitted it to the voters on December 21, 1857. It was a tricky document, for the voters did not vote for or against the constitution itself, but only whether they wanted to accept it with or without slavery.

By this time there were more free-state settlers living in Kansas than those who were pro-slavery in view. But even if the majority had voted for the constitution "without slavery," Kansas would still be a slave state. This was because there was a clause in the constitution which permitted all existing slavery in Kansas to continue. So "without slavery" meant only that no more slaves could be brought into the state. Because of this fraudulent situation the free-state men refused to vote, and the constitution was adopted "with slavery."

In February, 1858, President Buchanan sent the Lecompton Constitution to Congress and

recommended that it be accepted. Buchanan was
old and weak-willed. Although he was from Pennsylvania, he was completely controlled by the
Southerners in Congress and in his cabinet. He
had been persuaded to do everything in his power
to make Kansas a slave state.

Senator Douglas, however, was angered by
the contents of the Lecompton Constitution and
the way in which it had been adopted. It was
against the principle of his Kansas-Nebraska Bill
whereby *all* the people in a territory were to vote
on the issue of slavery. "The constitution is a
mockery and an insult," said Senator Douglas,
"and I will resist it to the last."

To protest the Lecompton Constitution,
Douglas called on the President and stated his
views.

But Buchanan was equally determined. "I wish
you to remember," he told Douglas, "that no
Democrat ever differed from the administration
without being crushed."

A threat of this kind did little to frighten
Douglas, who thought he was the strongest leader

in the Democratic party. "I wish you to remember, Mr. President," he answered, "that General Jackson is dead."

On the evening that Douglas spoke in the
Senate against the Lecompton Constitution, even
the corridors in the Capitol were crowded with
spectators. Each vigorous statement he made was
greeted with applause, though more from the
Republicans than the Democrats. "The constitution is not the act and the deed of the people of
Kansas," he said at the end of his speech, "and
therefore, I deny your right to make it into law."

In the front row of the visitor's gallery, sat
beautiful Adele Cutts Douglas, the Senator's second wife, whom he had married in 1856. She
was a highly intelligent girl though twenty years
younger than her husband. Perhaps, this was
because Dolly Madison was her great-aunt and
Adele might have learned finesse from her
charming relative.

There was no hostess in Washington more
gracious and well-liked than Adele Douglas. The
most influential people in politics and society

came to the parties which were constantly being
given now in the Douglas mansion on New
Jersey Avenue. The clothes Adele wore and
the way she entertained became the models for
Washington society. She was the first one to
draw the curtains and light candles when serv-
ing afternoon tea, and soon every hostess was
doing likewise.

But Adele's chief devotion was for her husband,
his children and their home. The Douglas boys
loved her dearly, and she was an ideal stepmother.
She was keenly interested in her husband's career
and listened in the Senate gallery to every speech
that he made.

As Douglas finished his speech on the Lecompton Constitution, Adele swiftly ran down the
steps from the gallery and tenderly wrapped a
shawl around his shoulders which were dripping
with perspiration. Perhaps this devotion and her
enthusiastic comments made Douglas confident
that he would win in the fight he would now
have with the President.

But Douglas was wrong. In spite of his protesting speeches, the Senate accepted the constitution. In the House, it was amended and then pigeon-holed. According to the amendment, the constitution itself without any qualifying clauses was to be submitted to the people of Kansas. This time the free-staters voted. The result was 1,926 votes for the constitution but 11,812 against it. The free-staters would rather have Kansas remain a territory than come in as a slave state.

And so the fate of Kansas remained undecided until after the Civil War had begun in 1861 when it was admitted as a free state.

But the fate of Senator Douglas grew steadily worse. The President vowed vengeance on this man who had dared to oppose him. Every federal officer who had supported Douglas was dismissed. Democratic newspapers which shared the views of the Senator lost government patronage, and many failed as a result. The hatred of Buchanan for Douglas never ceased.

8. A House Divided

ABRAHAM LINCOLN'S RIGHT SIDE WAS hunched against the front of the battered writing desk in his office. His long legs were stretched on a chair in front of him. His left arm dangled rakelike to the floor. As he carefully wrote with an old-fashioned quill pen on the big sheets of paper spread out on the desk, his lips moved and he muttered half-aloud the words he was writing. Since his childhood days in the "blab" school in Kentucky, he had always repeated aloud what he read or wrote. It was Saturday afternoon in early June, 1858. He and his partner, William Herndon, were alone in their office.

Lincoln and Herndon shared two small rooms

in one of the three-story brick buildings that faced the square in Springfield. On the ground floor was a cutlery store. To get to the offices, one climbed a steep wooden stairway and walked down a dark narrow corridor. In the front room clients waited, while the back room was a private office. Here, in addition to the old desk, were two oak tables covered with green baize, a few scuffed wooden chairs, and a bookcase with about two hundred law books.

In the corner, was Lincoln's bulging old cotton umbrella with its hooked handle and "A. Lincoln" neatly inscribed on the inside. On the desk was an iron letter press. When the partners wanted to have an extra copy of a written paper, they put the freshly written document on the press, placed a sheet of thin paper over it, revolved the screw of the press until it was tight, and in a few seconds would have a copy.

The office rooms were seldom cleaned. Once, shortly after Lincoln had come back from Washington with packages of garden seeds for his friends, a new law student got out a broom and swept up the floor, for the seeds which had fallen were sprouting in the dark corners of the room.

But there were no law students or even clients in the waiting room this afternoon. Lincoln was writing the most important speech of his career up to that time. It was his acceptance of the Republican nomination for the office of senator from Illinois. The nominating convention would not be held until June 16th, but Lincoln was sure to be the candidate.

Occasionally, as Lincoln worked at his desk, he would take a scribbled-over scrap of paper or back of an envelope from the inside band of his worn stovepipe hat. It was turned upside down on the desk and was used, as always, to file letters and memoranda. With lips tightened, he jabbed a final period on the last sheet of paper and looked toward his partner.

"It's finished, Billy. Want to hear it?"

Herndon glanced up from the brief he had been copying at the ink-stained center table.

"That's why I've been waiting, Mr. Lincoln."
They were always "Billy" and "Mr. Lincoln."

"I suppose I shouldn't let the whole world
know I've written an acceptance speech before
I've been chosen," said Lincoln, grinning as he
locked the office door and drew the grimy curtain
over the glass pane in the doorway. "But I've
been thinking about this speech for a long time."

Herndon nodded. He knew that the speech
would contain Lincoln's views on the slavery
question. Herndon himself was an Abolitionist.
He didn't know why. "I feel it in my bones," he
said. Lincoln said that was his partner's "bone
philosophy."

Lincoln went back to the desk, shifted the
papers until they were in a neat pile, then swung
one long leg over the other. Slowly and emphat-
ically he began to read. His voice was high-
pitched and strident, and he spoke with the twang
of the Kentucky mountaineers, so that he said
"thar" and "git" and "sich." But this was of little
importance to Herndon.

Lincoln scribbled away on his acceptance speech.

"If we could first know where we are and whither we are tending, we could better judge what to do and how to do it," read Lincoln. "We are now far into the fifth year since a policy was initiated with the avowed object and confident promise of putting an end to slavery agitation. Under the operation of that policy, that agitation not only has not ceased, but has constantly augmented. In my opinion, it will not cease until a crisis shall have been reached and passed. 'A house divided against itself cannot stand.' I believe this government cannot endure permanently half slave and half free. I do not expect the Union to be dissolved—I do not expect the house to fall—but I do expect it will cease to be divided. It will become all one thing or all the other. Either the opponents of slavery will arrest the further spread of it, and place it where the public mind shall rest in the belief that it is in the course of ultimate extinction; or its advocates will push it forward, till it shall become lawful in all states, old as well as new, North as well as South."

Lincoln stopped and looked at his partner over his spectacles. He had been using them for the past half dozen years, but only to read.

Herndon whistled softly. "What you say is true. But is it wise to use that 'house divided' expression?"

"It's a universally known figure of speech," Lincoln argued. "I think it will strike home and make men realize the peril of these times." He paused and stared for a minute through the dusty windows at the Capitol building. "I would rather be defeated with this expression in the speech, than be victorious without it," he stated. "Now, I'll read you the rest."

The high-pitched voice continued with no further interruptions from Herndon. It was one of the finest and simplest speeches to which he had ever listened. Lincoln read no history or fiction. Only the Bible and Shakespeare beside his law books. And poetry. He liked Bobby Burns next to Shakespeare. He memorized and often repeated the verses he cherished. And so this speech had been written with the dignity and simplicity of the Bible, and the balance and music of the poems the writer enjoyed.

A few days later, Lincoln read the speech to some friends in the library of the State House. Herndon was among those present. He was the only one who approved the speech. The rest thought it was a "fool utterance" which would drive votes away from their candidate.

But Lincoln was persistent. "This thing has been retarded long enough," said he. "If it is decreed that I shall go down because of this speech, then let me go down linked to the truth."

"If you deliver that speech, Mr. Lincoln," said Herndon, "it will make you President."

Lincoln smiled a little. His partner sounded like Mary who was always saying that some day her husband would be President.

The rest of the men were grimly silent. They still intended to nominate Lincoln for the senatorship, but they doubted if he would win the election.

Douglas's car was trimmed with flags and mottoes.

"I shall have my hands full," remarked Douglas when he heard that Lincoln had been nominated for the senatorship of Illinois by the Republicans. "Abraham Lincoln is the strongest man of his party. He is as honest as he is shrewd, and if I can beat him, my victory will be hardly won."

But other Democrats laughed at the idea of this gangling, uncouth local politician, the nominee of a new party, having even a chance against the man who was the strongest leader of a party long established and now dominant in the nation. What was more, Republicans in the East, like Greeley, were suggesting to the Republicans in Illinois that they join with the Democrats and back Douglas because of his stand on the Lecompton Constitution.

By horsedrawn vehicle, steamboat and train, the two candidates began traveling through Illinois. Douglas usually rode in an open carriage drawn by white horses. Mrs. Douglas went with him on all his trips, looking her loveliest. She was a charming vote-getter for her husband.

When Douglas traveled by train, it was in a special car decorated with flags and mottoes. Attached to this was a flatcar carrying two brass cannons and an escort of young men dressed in semi-military fashion. The cannons boomed. The

118

crowds cheered. In every town, there was a big demonstration.

Often Lincoln traveled on the same train, though in one of the public cars. When he went to meetings, to emphasize the pioneer background of their candidate, he and his followers rode in a Conestoga wagon drawn by six white horses. Except for one meeting in Alton, Mary Lincoln remained at home in Springfield with the children.

Toward the end of July, Lincoln made a request of Douglas. "Will it be agreeable to you," wrote Lincoln, "to make an arrangement for us to address the same audiences?"

Reluctantly Douglas accepted the offer. He was not afraid to meet Lincoln in debate, but he knew that the meetings would add to the importance of his opponent.

The challenge, however, was a bold step for Lincoln. Douglas was the ablest debater in the country. He had charm of manner and much personal attraction. In debate, he was vigorous and bold, and expert at getting out of tight corners. He could disarm an opponent with a graceful compliment as well as a telling point.

Nevertheless, seven towns in the Congressional districts where neither man so far had spoken were selected for meeting places, and thus began the "great debates."

9. Who Is This Man Lincoln?

WHEN LINCOLN GOT OFF THE TRAIN AT Freeport, Illinois, for his second debate with Douglas, the brass band blared and the crowd pressed forward to greet him. His worn stovepipe hat was pushed back a little on his rumpled black hair. He wore a rather shabby store-bought black alpaca suit with sleeves too short to cover his big, bony wrists, and with tight trousers that showed the tops of his boots. His neck looked even more lean and sinewy in the white shirt he wore with its low collar and narrow black silk bow tie.

Through the streets of the town went the welcoming parade, with little bands tooting at every corner. Flags fluttered from the balconies and housetops, and the closed stores were gay with bunting and placards. Everybody was in holiday dress. Thousands of people had come by special train, and hundreds of farm families had ridden in wagons and buggies, bringing their lunch and making a picnic of the occasion. Douglas and his wife had arrived the preceding evening, and there had been the usual demonstration.

About noon a drizzling rain started, but it had little effect on the high spirits of the crowd. The debate was to be held near the center of town, for there were fifteen thousand people in Freeport that day. The program would begin promptly at two o'clock. Lincoln would speak for one hour. Douglas would have one hour and a half to answer Lincoln's statements. Then Lincoln would have one half hour to close the debate. In the preceding meeting at Ottawa, the order of speaking had been the reverse. Timekeepers, watch in hand, checked carefully, and neither speaker was allowed an extra second, except to finish a sentence.

There was an important question that Lincoln planned to ask in the debate that day. He wanted to put Douglas in a sharply anti-slavery position and thus weaken his following in the South. His plan was to show that Douglas upheld the Dred Scott decision which denied to *Congress* the power to make laws regarding slavery, and at the same time sponsored the doctrine of "popular sovereignty" in his Kansas-Nebraska Law which gave the *people of a territory* the right to make such laws.

Lincoln knew how Douglas would defend his position. He would say that the people of a territory did not have more power than Congress. However, they could prevent slavery from spreading by passing laws that would make it unprofitable for a slaveholder to settle in their territory. But Lincoln wanted Douglas to make that statement in a joint debate where both sides of the argument could be heard.

The night before at a hotel stop, and on the train coming to Freeport, Lincoln had discussed the question with his political friends. They had been opposed. They thought that it would give Douglas the chance to talk himself out of a difficult situation and thus win more votes.

"If you ask that question, you will never be elected senator from Illinois," they told him.

"Gentlemen, I am killing larger game," answered Lincoln, as determined as he had been in the "house divided" speech. "If Douglas answers as I think he will, he can never be President. The battle of 1860 is worth a hundred of this."

Lincoln rode out to the meeting in his Conestoga wagon, but Douglas decided to walk. He could be as down-to-earth as his opponent. Soon the speakers and the committee were on the platform, which was rather poorly sheltered from the rain.

Reporters were standing or sitting near the grandstand. They were taking down their accounts of the speech in their newly learned short-

Lincoln and Douglas were introduced to the crowd.

hand, so that they were able to give a detailed report. These stories were being reprinted in every important newspaper in the country, and for the first time a current event in the West was being fully recorded. "Who is this man Lincoln?" was the question now being asked in the East.

Cheering, shouting, jostling, eating and drinking, the crowd pressed close to the platform. The two speakers were introduced by the chairman. They both rose and bowed to the cheering onlookers. Never was there such a contrast!

Lincoln was six feet, four inches tall, though looking less when he stood stoop-shouldered as now. He was muscular and powerful, but his long arms dangled awkwardly, and his legs were like pipestems in their narrow, ill-fitting trousers. His clean-shaven face had deep furrows rather than wrinkles, and his skin was yellow and leathery in texture. His whole face had an air of deep melancholy, and his gray eyes seemed as dull as worn agates.

Bowing pleasantly, waving gracefully, stood Stephen A. Douglas who even though he was a foot shorter than Lincoln managed to look dignified. His linen shirt and high, white-winged collar gleamed in the gray light of the day. His blue broadcloth coat fitted perfectly. His whole face showed fight and audacity.

There were a few opening remarks; then Lincoln was ready to start the debate. He rose slowly, as if by inches, until like a lonely pine he was stretched to his full, ungainly height.

"Mr. Cheerman," he began. His voice was thin and shrill, his first words halting. The twang of Kentucky, as always, was in his accent. But somehow those strident tones could be heard in the last fringes of the crowd, and instantly there was silence.

First Lincoln answered the questions that Douglas had asked of him in his closing half-hour speech in Ottawa. As Lincoln spoke, his rawboned figure seemed to grow less angular, and his stiff gestures became more natural. The words he uttered flowed easily and logically, and his face and eyes lit up as if with an inward glow.

There was no high humor in his talk. There were no light references and none of the stories for which he was famous. The question of whether slavery should be extended or not was serious for Lincoln, and this was the only topic discussed by the two men in their debates.

Next Lincoln asked his own four questions. The second was the one so hotly discussed with his companions on the preceding night. "Can the people of a territory in any lawful way," he asked slowly, "exclude slavery prior to the formation of their own state constitution?"

"He's got him! He's got him now!" commented Lincoln's followers gleefully.

Two other related questions quickly followed. There was warm but short applause. Those who were present wanted to hear how Douglas would answer.

Lincoln wiped his perspiring face and sat down as Douglas walked to the front of the platform.

Smiling and at ease, apparently in no way disturbed, Douglas began to speak. His voice was rich and vibrant. It carried effortlessly to the edge of the crowd. With easy candor, he answered Lincoln's question much as he had done in speeches he had made before.

Yes, he said, a territory could exclude slavery by passing laws that were "unfriendly" to the institution, and explained his meaning. This became the "Freeport Doctrine" of "unfriendly legislation." It was a glib and momentary reply. The crowd thundering their amazed applause did not guess how far-reaching that answer would be. But in years to come that answer was remembered by the Southern Democrats who refused to support Stephen Douglas.

Election day in Illinois that year was on November 2, 1858. Rain fell all day long. At this time, senators were not elected directly by the people but by the state legislatures. So the people did not vote for the candidates for senatorship but for the legislators who favored them.

When the votes were counted, Lincoln had 125,-275 popular votes and Douglas had 121, 090. But because the districts were not divided in proportion to the population, Douglas received the votes of fifty-four legislators to Lincoln's forty-six. So Douglas won the election.

"Let the voice of the people rule," was the answer of Douglas to the telegram sent to him in Washington to announce his victory.

When Lincoln was asked how he felt, he said he was like the boy who had stubbed his toe. "It hurt too bad to laugh, and he was too big to cry."

However, Lincoln did not let defeat make him lose interest in politics. As he wrote to a friend, the "fizzle gigs and fireworks" were over, but the campaign had been good fun. "Another blow-up is coming, and we shall have fun again." He was thinking of that bigger "battle" in 1860.

One more dramatic incident was to happen to weld the North into a solid band of opposition to the spread of slavery.

At eight o'clock on the night of Sunday,

October 16, 1859, a horse-drawn wagon crossed the covered bridge from the Maryland side of the Potomac River to Harpers Ferry, Virginia. There were about eighteen men in the wagon under the leadership of John Brown, white-bearded now, but still slender and commanding in appearance, and still fanatically intent on destroying slavery. Tonight, he hoped, would bring to a successful conclusion a strange and involved plot.

A year before, Brown had met some of his old Abolitionist friends in the home of Gerrit Smith, a wealthy Abolitionist leader of New York, and had told them of his plan. Brown proposed setting up a stronghold in Virginia where Abolitionists, freed Negroes, and fugitive slaves could join him. They would make guerrilla attacks on the neighboring plantations, until Brown's name would become a scourge and the planters would feel so insecure that they would sell their slaves even at a loss. The procedure would spread all over the country, and thus slavery would be brought to an end.

The plan was foolhardy, but Brown was obstinate and still had complete faith in the words of the Bible. "Joshua took a walled city by the blowing of trumpets and the shouts of the people," he argued. "God will not forsake me."

"We cannot let our friend die alone," said Gerrit Smith and gave Brown money.

Eventually, $14,000 was raised and used to buy Sharps rifles, revolvers, and pikes, which were two-edged pieces of metal on a six-foot pole. The pikes were for the slaves who had never been permitted to learn the use of arms. "Give a slave a pike and he will become a man," Brown promised.

In July, 1859, Brown with two of his sons and some followers rented a farm on the Maryland side of the Potomac about five miles from Harpers Ferry, a town in what was then Virginia. The town lies at the junction of the Potomac and Shenandoah Rivers. A United States arsenal was located in Harpers Ferry.

At the farm, Brown collected the supplies he

Fighting broke out in the streets of Harpers Ferry.

needed. No one suspected him. He was thought
to be buying sheep for his wool business. Much
of his planning was secret and involved. Only
one of his backers knew of his real intention
which was to capture the United States arsenal
and use it as a point of attack.

Once the covered bridge was crossed on the
night of October 16th, the plan moved quickly
and at first successfully. At the arsenal, the
civilian watchmen were easily overcome. Forag-

ing parties were sent to free the neighborhood slaves and bring them to the armory. Prominent plantation owners were captured to be held as hostages. One was Lewis Washington, General Washington's great-grandnephew. Lewis Washington possessed the sword given to General Washington by Frederick the Great, and Brown wanted that sword for himself.

At dawn, the citizens of Harpers Ferry slowly became aware of what had happened in their town. Some were captured on their way to work, so that by noon on Monday, there were about fifty prisoners in the arsenal. Soon the neighboring militia arrived, and real fighting began. Brown and his followers and captives retired to the small brick engine house in the yard of the arsenal.

Hour by hour, Brown's position grew more hopeless. One of his sons was dead and the other mortally wounded. Brown, who also was severely wounded, knelt between both of his sons. In one hand he held his gun ready for firing. With the other hand, he felt the pulse of his dying son. The prisoners huddled together in a corner, their liberated slaves making no effort to fight. Some of the Negroes even helped their captured masters. The possession of pikes had not made fighting men of the slaves.

Monday evening, eighty Marines arrived under the command of Colonel Robert E. Lee of the United States Army. On Tuesday morning, when Brown refused to surrender, the Marines battered down the door of the engine house with a ladder and took the inmates captive.

The seven men who had not been killed or managed to escape were immediately indicted. Brown refused to name his backers and assumed the entire blame. The trial took place early in November. Governor Wise of Virginia knew that if he waited, he would not be able to prevent a lynching.

Prominent lawyers came to Brown's defense. He was brought into court on a couch, for he was too weak to sit up for his trial. His lawyers tried to plead insanity, but Brown insisted he was sane. "Treason and conspiracy and advising with slaves and others to rebel," was the charge against him, and the sentence was death by hanging on December 2, 1859. The trial was fair, said Brown, though he "felt no consciousness of guilt."

On the morning of his execution, John Brown rode calmly to the gallows. The day was bright and clear. He looked up at the sky before he mounted the platform. "This is a beautiful country," said he, then walked up the steps with steady tread.

In the South, there was horror and indignation and an effort to prove that the plot had been inspired by the Republicans. Many people in the North were equally horrified, and the Republicans would have nothing to do with the case.

But the poets and the philosophers of New England were less cautious. They were not obliged, said Thoreau scornfully, "to count the votes of Pennsylvania and company." Bells tolled in church steeples throughout the North and religious services were held in Boston on the day of the execution. Brown was "Christ crucified" or "Saint John the Just" to the literary people of New England.

In March, 1862, as a regiment from Massachusetts passed through Harpers Ferry, they paused at the little brick engine house which John Brown had tried to hold and sang a song which a quartet from their group had composed.

> *"John Brown's body lies a-mouldering*
> *in the ground,*
> *But his soul goes marching on."*

It was many years before that song ceased to have its impact of bitterness in both North and South.

10. The Taste Is in My Mouth a Little

THE BIGGER "BATTLE" TO WHICH ABRAHAM Lincoln had referred when campaigning for the senatorship in 1858 was the nomination for the presidency in 1860. At the time Lincoln made the statement, he had no thought that he might win that prize. His chief objective was to turn the South against Douglas so that he would not be nominated by the Democrats. For if Douglas were nominated, he was almost certain to win the election.

The President was nominated in 1860 much as he is today. Each party has a convention in some large city at which the platform of the party is

138

adopted and candidates are selected for the presidency and vice-presidency. The number of delegates to the convention from each state is determined largely by the number of its senators and representatives. The territories and other possessions of the United States also send delegates. Each is entitled to one vote. If a state sends double the number of its delegates, each is entitled to one half vote.

As a rule, the first order of business of a convention after the credentials of the delegates have been examined, is to adopt the rules for the convention. Then follow the discussion and vote on the platform which has been drawn up by a special committee. After this comes the nomination and then the balloting for the President, followed by the same procedure for the Vice-President.

For the nominations and the balloting, the secretary of the convention calls the states in alphabetical order, beginning with Alabama. The chairman from each state polls his delegates and announces the return. Sometimes the result is questioned, and then a delegate insists that the polling be done by the secretary of the convention. You may recall this if you watched or listened to the national conventions in 1952. A simple majority vote will nominate a Republican candidate, but before 1936, the Democrats required a two-thirds majority. At times this made the Democratic convention a long drawn-out contest.

It was so when the Democrats met on April 23, 1860, for their convention in Charleston, South Carolina, the most aristocratic city in the South. Northern delegates who had never been in the South before gaped at the luxurious mansions, the richly dressed women driving in elegant carriages and the gentlemen in wide-brimmed hats, spotless linen, and carrying gold-headed canes. On the other hand, the delegates were shocked to find themselves so close to the slave auction block.

Douglas seemed to be the only possible candidate. But the Southern "fire eaters" would not

agree to his principle of "popular sovereignty."
When it was adopted as the platform of the party,
the delegates from Alabama led by tall, dark-
haired William Yancey, walked out of the meeting. With them went the delegates from South
Carolina, Georgia, Florida, Mississippi, Texas,
Louisiana and Arkansas.

Fifty-seven ballots were taken, but Douglas
could not get the necessary two-thirds majority.
The convention then adjourned to meet in Baltimore on June 18th. Before that date, two other
conventions had been held. On May 9th, a new
organization, the Constitutional Union Party, met
and nominated John Bell of Tennessee. The members were mostly old-line Whigs who had not
already joined either the Republican or Democratic parties. They pledged themselves to protect the Union and to preserve the Constitution.
They took no stand on the question of slavery.
On May 16th, the Republican convention began
about noon in Chicago.

Before eleven o'clock the crowd in Chicago

was already edging its way toward the "Wig-wam," a huge, hastily built frame structure. It was the first building ever erected for a political convention. It had cost five thousand dollars to build and would hold ten thousand people. But thirty thousand wanted to get inside that day.

At half-past eleven, the three twenty-foot doors were cautiously opened, and the doorkeepers struggled to admit only ticket holders. Flags, festoons of bunting, and giant sprays of evergreen hid the bare walls of the interior. The ladies of Chicago had done the decorating and had been rewarded with tickets to the balcony. The only gentlemen admitted to the balcony were the escorts of the ladies. So school girls and a laundress were bribed a quarter to permit some male to go with them to the balcony. Even an Indian squaw who was selling moccasins near the Wigwam tried to enter on the same terms, but the doorkeeper kept her out because she was "no lady."

For months, the names of the Republican party leaders had been in the news. There were William

H. Seward of New York, governor and senator; Salmon P. Chase of Ohio and Simon Cameron of Pennsylvania, both senators; Edward Bates of Missouri, well-known judge; and Abraham Lincoln of Illinois, "neither judge nor senator, but plain citizen."

Mrs. Lincoln had always insisted that her husband was going to be a senator and then President. But he had laughed at her predictions. Inwardly, though, Lincoln must have hoped that his wife was correct. To have his name connected with important events of the time "is all that I desire to live for," he once said. Shortly before the Chicago convention, he had written to Lyman Trumbull, the Republican senator from Illinois, "At your request I'll be entirely frank. The taste is in my mouth a little."

A week before the convention, the Republicans of Illinois had met in Decatur and unanimously chosen Lincoln to be their candidate. Shortly before this, John Hanks, who was Lincoln's cousin, recalled that in 1830 he had helped the

Lincoln family build a cabin near Decatur when they had migrated to Illinois. Hanks and Abraham Lincoln had made a rail fence of native trees.

Hanks drove to the clearing with a friend, located two of the logs he and Lincoln had cut, and brought them back to Decatur. Then, while the state convention was in session, Hanks came into the hall with the two rails draped with flags and a banner, "Abraham Lincoln, the Rail Candidate for President in 1860. Two rails from a lot of 3000 made in 1830 by John Hanks and Abe Lincoln."

"Identify your work! Identify your work!" shouted the genial crowd.

A slow smile spread over Lincoln's face. He looked at the logs. They were honey locust and black walnut. Lasting timber. "It may be that I split these rails," he drawled. "But I must say that I've split a great many that were better looking."

But the "rail splitter" candidate was baptized that day, and the title gave him the homely simplicity that helped him in his campaign.

They paraded with two rails that Lincoln had split.

Lincoln decided to remain in Springfield during the convention in Chicago. At the Tremont House, his headquarters in Chicago, his campaign managers headed by Judge David Davis and Joseph Medill, publisher of *The Chicago Tribune*, were securing the votes of delegates by promising them "everything they asked."

"I authorize no bargains and will be bound by none," Lincoln had telegraphed his managers. But Judge Davis brushed that aside with, "Lincoln ain't here and don't know what we have to meet. We'll go ahead as if we hadn't heard from him."

At the Richmond House on Michigan Avenue, Seward's campaign manager was Thurlow Weed, a master politician. He had brought Dodsworth's Band with him. They were a thousand strong, and were dressed in brilliant uniforms with gold epaulets and red and white feathers waving from their caps. Up and down Michigan Avenue they paraded, playing Seward's campaign song, "Oh, Isn't He a Darling!"

Every train that brought delegates was met by the Wide Awakes, a marching organization that had been started when Lincoln was touring New England after his debates with Douglas. In Hartford, Connecticut, two of the young men who were escorting him decided they must do something to protect their clothing from the oil drippings of the kerosene torches they carried. They got pieces of oilcloth to put over their caps and make capes for their shoulders. The marshal of the parade thought this so practical that he placed them in the front rank. It was not long before young men all over the country were organizing themselves into clubs which they called "Wide Awakes," and adopting an oilcloth cape and glazed cap for a uniform.

Besides making promises and having parades there were other methods to influence delegates. All of the managers hired "shouters," but the Lincoln men had been given half rates on the Illinois railroads. They had been well trained, too, in the art of shouting. Joseph Medill directed them from the stage like an orchestra leader, though using a handkerchief instead of a baton.

Thurlow Weed, Seward's campaign manager, had good arguments for his candidate. The Democratic party was split, said Weed. This was the big chance for the Republican party. A man with the experience and ability of Seward could carry the country. Furthermore, the businessmen of the East were back of him. "Where will you get the money for the campaign if you don't back Seward?" seemed Weed's best argument.

But there were more important objections to Seward. He was considered too radical in his views on slavery, for he wished it to be abolished. As a result, Republicans in Pennsylvania, New Jersey, Illinois, and Indiana would not vote for him, and the votes of these states were needed to win the election. These were the four states in the North which had voted for Buchanan in 1856, and so were the ones in which the Republican party was weakest. Only a Republican candidate who was conservative would have a chance to win their votes.

Equal to Weed in influence at the convention was Horace Greeley, editor of *The New York Tribune*. He looked more like a curious farmer than a politician with his mild blue eyes behind silver-rimmed glasses, his round red and white face, and his scraggly fringe of whiskers. Greeley was bitterly opposed to Seward, and wanted Bates of Missouri to be nominated.

"How about Lincoln of Illinois?" a reporter asked him.

The band paraded up and down Michigan Avenue.

But the editor shook his head. "He's a clever politician with plenty of friends in the West, but he's had no national experience. Lincoln is too risky. Bates is safer."

During the first two days of the convention, the platform was drawn up. In regard to slavery, the Republicans stood for no further extension of the system but not abolition. Then on May 18th, the nominations began. Unlike today when long orations are made to nominate a candidate, the speeches were limited to one sentence. At last came the turn of Norman B. Judd. "I desire on behalf of the delegates from Illinois," he shouted, "to put in nomination as a candidate for President of the United States, Abraham Lincoln of Illinois."

Up went the hats of the men in a black cloud. The waving handkerchiefs of the ladies made a silver lining. The shouts were frantic, wild and shrill. "Like all the hogs ever slaughtered in Cincinnati giving their death squeal, plus a score of big steam whistles," as one reporter wrote.

There were 465 delegates, so that 233, a simple majority, were all that were necessary for a vote. On the first ballot, Seward had 173½ votes, Lincoln 102, and the rest were scattered. Switching of votes began with the second ballot. Seward received 184½ votes and Lincoln 181.

As is the case now in a national convention, each group of state delegates is usually "instructed" to vote for a certain candidate, at least on the first ballot. Today, most states have a "primary" or first election before the date of the convention. At this election, the individual members of each party vote for their choice of a candidate for their party. This choice determines the initial vote of the delegates. They may change later to another candidate, either because they have been instructed to do so, or because of their own decision. Often, to bring about this switch in a vote, the campaign managers make promises to the delegates, so that they will gain some political advantage either for themselves or their state.

The big increase in the vote for Lincoln on

the second ballot was of tremendous significance. It indicated that his campaign managers had persuaded delegates that Lincoln was a better second choice for them than was Seward.

"Call the roll! Call the roll!" was almost hissed by the delegates as soon as the returns of the second ballot were officially announced. They were eager to begin the third count.

As each state answered the third roll call and changes were noted, a whisper began to swell through the hall. "Lincoln's the man! He'll be nominated on this ballot!"

Hundreds of pencils had been marking the tally sheets, and delegates already knew the result. Up—up—up went Lincoln's count. Only one and a half more votes were needed to make the 233.

There was a profound silence. The fluttering of the ladies' fans ceased, and the whispering voices died out. One could hear the scratching of reporters' pens and the clicking of the telegraph keys. Then David Cartter of Ohio stood on his chair so that he could be seen. "Mr. Chairman," he yelled, "I rise to announce the change of four votes of Ohio from Mr. Chase to Mr. Lincoln."

There was a half minute of sudden quiet. A deep breath of relief. Then a noise like a rush of wind as the storm broke in the room. The man who was peering through a skylight got the prearranged signal that Lincoln was nominated, and a single cannon on the roof of the Wigwam roared out the news to the crowd in the streets. A hundred guns echoed from the roof of the Tremont Hotel. Only the puffs of smoke drifting past the windows of the Wigwam and the smell of gunpowder told this to the roaring crowd inside.

Steam whistles shrilled on the river boats and in the railroad yards. Church bells rang all over the city. A mad, hoarse crowd shouted and sang. For twenty-four hours there were tar barrels burning, drums beating, bands playing, fireworks bursting, and boys carrying rails and building bonfires.

Inside the Wigwam, delegates stood on chairs and strove to be recognized by the chairman of the convention so that they could change their votes to Lincoln. "Getting on the band wagon" —that is, being among those who vote for a successful candidate—was just as important to a politician then as now. At last Evarts, the chairman of the New York delegation, even though he was for Seward, courteously suggested that the nomination of Lincoln be made unanimous. Even as today, the political party, at least when it chooses a candidate, wishes to show harmony in the party.

How much effect the shouting had on the delegates to the Republican convention in 1860 cannot be estimated. They were serious men, well aware that this was a crucial election. Their switch to Lincoln was the result of careful consideration. He was chosen not so much because of his strength but rather because of the weakness of his opponents. Seward had been long in public life and had made enemies. He and Chase were considered too radical in their views. Lincoln was a new man in the party and with few enemies, and he had a middle-of-the-road view on slavery. He had the best chance to carry the four doubtful states and their votes were necessary to win the election.

In the afternoon session, Hannibal Hamlin of Maine was nominated for the vice-presidency. Shortly after, with "cheers for the ticket, the platform, and the ladies of Chicago," the convention was adjourned.

Later when Judge Davis was asked what it had cost to nominate Lincoln, he replied, "The entire expense including the headquarters, telegraphing, music, fare of delegates, and other incidentals was less than seven hundred dollars." The paid shouters were evidently included among the "incidentals."

On June 18th, when the Democrats met again in Baltimore, the delegates who had walked out of the convention at Charleston now asked for re-admission. Once more the argument arose concerning the platform. Once more the Southern delegates bolted the convention.

After the Southerners had withdrawn, the balloting began. This time, Douglas received nearly all the votes of those who were present and was declared the nominee of the party. The Southerners immediately held another convention in Baltimore and nominated John Breckinridge of Kentucky. Their platform stated that slavery should be protected in all parts of the United States.

And so the campaign started with four candidates—Douglas for the Northern Democrats; Breckenridge for the Southern Democrats; Lincoln for the Republicans; and Bell for the Constitutional Union Party. Of them all, Lincoln had the best chance to win. But should no candidate get the majority of the electoral votes, according to the Constitution, the election would be made by the House of Representatives.

In an election of this kind, each state has one vote, no matter how large or small it may be. Therefore, Breckinridge might win, for all the Southern states would vote for him, whereas the vote in the North might be divided.

A long, hard-fought campaign was to take place.

11. *Here I Have Lived*

It was hard for Lincoln not to be restless during the three days of the convention. He wanted to behave as usual, but at home, in his law office, and in the streets there was only one thing being discussed. Who would be nominated?

On Thursday, he tried to bowl and later on to play billiards but both the alleys and tables were all engaged. In the afternoon, he played a game of "fives," like handball today, and loosened the tension in his muscles and in his spirit.

Friday morning he gave up all pretense. First, he went to his office where friends soon brought in telegrams stating the situation. They decided then to go to the telegraph office and hear the news more quickly. Men were crowded around the operator's table listening breathlessly each time the little instrument clicked.

News of the first ballot came over the wire. Lincoln thought it favorable. Then came the returns of the second ballot.

"I've got him," said Lincoln reaching for his hat. "Let's go over to the *Journal*."

In single file the men clattered down the narrow stairway of the building. Some of them lingered to announce the news to the crowd already assembled in the square.

Hats started to fly. There were cheers. "Abe's got him! Abe's got him!" was the cry.

At twelve o'clock came the news of the nomination. The operator was so excited that he threw down his pencil and yelled. Then he quickly copied the telegram, "Abe we did it. Glory be to God!" and ran across the square waving the dispatch.

Those in the *Journal* office heard the wild cheering and came down. Everybody pressed forward to shake the hand of the candidate, to

News of the first ballot came over the wire.

slap him on the back, and to wish him success. "Three cheers for our next President!" came the cry.

"We'll have to write a book about you," someone shouted.

"It seems to me there isn't much in my past life to write a book about," Lincoln answered.

Outwardly he seemed to be calm. Inwardly he felt a little sick. Although the day was warm, the tiny beads of perspiration on his forehead and upper lip felt cold. It was a long way for a man to come. Log cabin in Kentucky—the Indiana lean-to—storekeeper in New Salem—the self-taught lawyer—at last, step by step up the political ladder.

Then he looked in the direction of his house and began to ease away from the crowd. "Well, gentlemen," said he. "There is a little woman at home who is probably more interested in this dispatch than I am. If you will excuse me, I'll take it up to her and let her see it."

The next evening, a committee came to the house on Eighth and Jackson Streets in Springfield formally to notify Lincoln of his nomination. Lincoln was waiting in the parlor on the left side of the entrance hall. It was a neat and pleasant room and furnished like most middle-class homes of the day.

For a while after the formal notification, the

conversation was strained. Then Lincoln commented on the height of one man, and they stood shoulder to shoulder to measure heights. After that, Lincoln's "That reminds me," started one of his stories, and soon they were all repeating news about the convention, much of which Lincoln already knew, but all of which he was eager to hear again. The committee, several of whom were Easterners, left feeling more confident. Now began the fight to win.

Douglas was the only candidate in 1860 who took an active part in the campaign. He was confident that the election of Lincoln would bring about secession, and he pleaded with the people of the North not to vote the Republican ticket. But the threat of secession had been made so often that it was like a cry of "Wolf!"

Once in Norfolk, Virginia, someone asked Douglas if he thought that the South had the right to secede if Lincoln were elected.

"By no means," answered Douglas candidly.

"And has the President the right to stop secession?"

"It is the President's duty to preserve the Union," answered Douglas gravely. "And it is my duty and your duty to do all in our power to aid him."

That ended any chance of Douglas's getting votes in the South.

Lincoln remained in Springfield during the whole campaign. The Governor's Room in the State House was set aside for him, and here he went each morning with his young law student, John Nicolay, to act as secretary. Here also came the artists to paint Lincoln's portrait and newsmen to write his biography.

However, there was vigorous campaigning for Lincoln elsewhere. The nights were a-glitter with burning tar barrels, fireworks, and bonfires. The Wide Awakes and men bearing fence rails marched in parade singing their campaign song:

Old Abe Lincoln came out of the wilderness
Out of the wilderness, out of the wilderness.
Old Abe Lincoln came out of the wilderness,
Down in Illinois.

163

The literary men of New England wrote poems and made impassioned speeches. There was one rail-splitting battalion in Boston where each member was at least six feet, two inches tall.

But it was the young people who were most active and enthusiastic. They had read *Uncle Tom's Cabin*. They were not held down by political traditions. The campaign was their crusade, and a country rid of slavery was their Holy Land. The boys from twelve to eighteen who could not vote had their own marching club called "Hickory Buds."

Election Day was on November 6, 1860. The day was bright with sunshine in Springfield. At first, Lincoln had decided not to vote. Then he realized that there were other officers being elected, so he cut off the list of presidential electors and voted the rest of the ticket. Late in the afternoon, he crossed the square to the court house and amid a cheering crowd cast his ballot.

There are two types of votes cast for a candidate in a presidential election, the popular vote and the electoral vote. The people do not vote directly for the President but for electors who will vote for him officially the following January. Each party has as many electors in a state as there are senators and representatives. According to what is known as the "unit rule" the entire electoral vote of the state goes to whichever party gets the majority of votes in a state. That is why the votes cast in the large states are considered so important.

Returns for the election in 1860 began coming in about nine o'clock to the little telegraph office in Springfield where Lincoln and his friends waited. With each favorable report, which at first came from the North, the excitement grew. Then dispatches not so favorable came from the South. "It's time they got a few licks in," said Lincoln philosophically.

"New York will settle it," Lyman Trumbull predicted.

It was almost midnight before the news came from New York. For a moment, the operator was so excited that he couldn't read the message aloud. Then one of the men grabbed the dispatch and ran out to the square. " 'Spatch! 'Spatch! New York!" he cried breathlessly, but everyone knew what he meant.

Ten thousand people screamed madly, threw their hats in the air, slapped each other's backs, started bonfires, lighted torches, began to parade, blared forth from their band instruments, or sang their campaign song.

But Abraham Lincoln turned and said quietly to Trumbull, "I guess I'll go home and tell Mary about it."

On the morning of February 11, 1861, the President-to-be was waiting at the Chenery Hotel in Springfield for the carriage which was to take him to the railroad station. The family had been living there during their last few days in the town. Robert, the oldest boy who had come home from Harvard after the nomination, was to go on the train with his father. Mary and the

younger children were to join them the next day
in Indianapolis.

So much had happened. So much had to be
done before this last day in Springfield. The re-
ceptions, portrait painting, and biographies had
continued. Lincoln had his inauguration address
to write and his cabinet to appoint. He visited
his beloved stepmother, Sarah Bush Lincoln, near
Charleston, Illinois. He had made arrangements
with Herndon, who had decided not to go to
Washington, to continue their law practice.

The house on Eighth Street had been rented
and its furnishings sold or given away. Once a
neighbor had watched Mrs. Lincoln throwing
old letters and papers into a bonfire and had
begged for a few sheets. But much had been
destroyed.

Now everything was ready. Lincoln had tied
all the trunks with ropes and on each piece of
luggage had put one of the hotel cards with the
inscription, "A. Lincoln, the White House,
Washington, D. C." It was seven o'clock. Time

to go. A heavy rain was falling. For the last time, Abraham Lincoln peered through the rain-streaked windows of the carriage and saw all the familiar sights of Springfield and the people who were on the sidewalks to see him leave.

At the station, about a thousand people were gathered, and soldiers were lined up to protect him. Slowly he passed through the ranks, shaking hands, speaking a few words, nodding right and left. Hands reached out to touch his coat sleeve or the gray woolen shawl around his shoulders.

A special train of two cars had been provided. He was taking both his young law students, John Hay and John Nicolay, to be his personal secretaries. They did not get along with Mrs. Lincoln, which was too bad since they were all to live in the White House. But maybe with the excitement of being in Washington, the difficulties would end. Nicolay was as dependable as two times two, and Hay was a brilliant, charming young man. He would be good company for Robert Lincoln who looked very elegant this morning in his well-fitting frock coat, gray trousers, and high silk hat. Already the people were calling him, "The Prince of Rails."

Finally Lincoln mounted the train steps. He had not intended to make a speech. But seeing all these good people, gathered on this wet morning to see him off, tugged at his heart. He stood on the back platform of the train, dressed in his new black broadcloth suit and shiny silk hat. As usual, his coat hung loosely on his lean frame. He pulled the gray woolen shawl close and unconsciously stroked the whiskers on his chin. Early in January he had started to grow a beard. Some said this was because a little girl, Grace Bedell, had urged him to do so in a letter. The hair fringed his cheeks and covered the fine molding of his chin. But Mrs. Lincoln had approved. She thought the beard made him look more dignified.

Lincoln took off his hat and stroked it absently. The rest of the men doffed their hats. There was silence. Like a little prayer. Slowly Lincoln began to speak.

"Here I have lived a quarter of a century. Here my children have been born and one is buried. I now leave, not knowing when or whether ever I may return, with a task before me greater than that which rested on Washington. Trusting in Him who can go with me, and remain with you, and be everywhere for good, let us confidently hope that all will yet be well. . . . I now bid you an affectionate farewell."

The bell rang. The little square-topped smokestack of the engine puffed. The train gave a grinding jerk. Slowly, Lincoln entered the car while the people stood with heads bared.

"Good-bye! Good-bye!" they cried until the train was far down the track. Most of them would never see Abraham Lincoln again.

12. On to Washington

Fifteen men were in the Lincoln party that left Springfield for Washington, D. C. Judge David Davis, who was almost as wide as he was tall, was along; and tall, broad-shouldered Ward Hill Lamon. He was a handsome young Virginian from a wealthy, aristocratic family and he was Lincoln's law partner in Danville, Illinois. Lamon had brought his banjo with him on the trip; and almost the moment the train pulled out of the station, he was plucking the strings and everybody was singing old plantation songs.

About eleven o'clock on the second morning, Mrs. Lincoln and the younger boys joined the party at Indianapolis. It was her husband's fifty-third birthday, and she loved celebrating anniversaries too much to be separated from him on this day.

The train made leisurely progress through Indiana, Ohio, New York, New Jersey and Pennsylvania. The people of the East wanted to see their new President. The trip probably would take two weeks instead of a few days. Every town and village through which the train passed was decorated with flags and bunting, and the whole population turned out to see the presidential party.

At Westfield, New York, the train stopped so that Lincoln could kiss Grace Bedell, the little girl who had suggested that he grow whiskers. By this time they were full, and barbers were advertising a new cream called "Lincoln Whiskerophorer," which guaranteed to grow a beard in six weeks.

When the party reached Philadelphia, a young detective, Allan Pinkerton, assigned by the railroad to protect the President-to-be, had an alarming story to tell. There was a plot to assassinate

Lincoln if the train went through Baltimore as scheduled. An Italian barber, Ferrandini, was to rush on the train and kill him. Because Baltimore was pro-slavery, it would furnish no protection for the party.

Little Grace Bedell rushed up to greet Lincoln.

Colonel Sumner, in charge of Lincoln's military escort, sputtered indignantly. "I'll take a squad of cavalry and cut our way through," he promised.

But in the evening, Frederick Seward, the son of the Senator, came from Washington with word that his father also had learned of the plot. All through the night, therefore, elaborate plans were made by those in charge. Lincoln had insisted that he appear at the Harrisburg and Philadelphia ceremonies that were planned for the next day, and leave in the evening for Washington.

Shortly before six o'clock on the following day, a closed carriage drew up at a side door of the hotel in Harrisburg. Quietly excusing himself from the group at the dinner table, Lincoln hurried to his room and changed his clothes. With only big Ward Lamon for company, the President-to-be got into the carriage and drove to the railroad station where a special train took him back to Philadelphia. In the meantime, all the telegraph lines out of Harrisburg had been cut so that no news of his movements could be sent.

It was nearly ten o'clock when the train reached Philadelphia. No one recognized the tall man with a felt hat pulled down over his ears, and a gray woolen shawl drawn over his shoulders who hurried with a giant-sized companion to a waiting carriage. In it were Pinkerton and one of the railroad officials.

The train to Washington which would pass through Baltimore did not leave until midnight, so the four men drove around Philadelphia until nearly that time. Then they got aboard the train through a rear door. One of their group was "an invalid" was the explanation given, and they wanted to save him the walk through the cars

The oil lamps burned dimly in the green-curtained Pullman coach. Four berths had been reserved, but Lincoln was the only one to use his reservation. The others watched and waited tensely. A carefully sealed package marked "government dispatches" but containing old newspapers had been sent to the conductor. It was his signal to start the train.

The whistle blew. The train gave a jerk. The journey to Washington began. At each station, Pinkerton stepped off the train to send word that so far there was no trouble. All was quiet in the sleeping car except for occasional muffled laughter when Lincoln made some humorous remark. The berth was too short for his long frame and the intensity of the situation too great to permit peaceful slumber.

At three-thirty in the morning, the train moved slowly through the dark and quiet streets of Baltimore. The engine was changed. Cars were shifted. Once more the train moved on. Pinkerton slipped his gun back into its holster.

The unfinished dome of the Capitol showed in the gray morning light about six o'clock. A half hour later, the four passengers got off the train. Only Senator Seward was there to greet them. He had met every train from the North during the night.

That evening Senator Douglas called on the Lincolns.

They drove immediately to the Willard Hotel where the party was to stay until the inauguration. In the telegraph office, Pinkerton stopped to send a message. "Plums arrived here this morning with Nuts all right."

In the afternoon, the rest of the party arrived. They had traveled along the route planned, and there had been no incident. Perhaps this was because the news of the early arrival of Lincoln was now generally known. Perhaps there had been no plot at all, but a fine scheme to achieve notoriety developed by an enterprising young detective.

That evening Senator Stephen A. Douglas called on the family. Lincoln's face lighted as soon as Douglas came into the room. His hand reached out immediately. Once again the two opponents met. But there was no triumph in Lincoln's manner; no ill will on the part of Douglas.

There were the usual greetings and inquiries.

Mrs. Douglas would call on Mrs. Lincoln to-morrow, said the Senator. Mary's face brightened. Adele Douglas was the leader of Washington society. Her early call would set a pattern.

Douglas asked that he be allowed to join the presidential party at the inaugural ball. Perhaps Mrs. Lincoln would permit him to promenade with her. "We're more of a size," he said, grinning.

But Douglas, though charming and genial as always, soon let it be known that his call meant more than polite usage.

"You and I, sir," he said to Lincoln, "have differed politically many times. But in our attachment to the Union, we have never differed."

"God bless you, Douglas," said Lincoln. "You cheer and warm my heart."

"Should secession come," continued the Senator from Illinois gravely, "there will be only two parties, patriots and traitors. And I, sir, am a patriot."

The Little Giant and the Tall Giant from Illinois! In love of the Union, they were both of equal stature.

The first Republican contest for the presidency had been won. It had been fought on the issue of the extension of slavery. Eventually, it would bring about the emancipation of the slaves.

Even before Lincoln was inaugurated, seven of the Southern states had seceded and established a separate nation, the Confederate States of America. It would take four years of bloody struggle to restore those states to the Union, and many years of peaceful living to rebuild a united country.

Index

INDEX

LANDMARK BOOKS

WORLD LANDMARK BOOKS